# *Prophetic*
## *for 2019* *Words*

# *Prophetic*
## *for 2019* *Words*

*with contributions from…*

James Goll, Bill Hamon, Michael L. Brown, Patricia King, Lana Vawser, Robert Henderson, Charlie Shamp, Jennifer LeClaire, Nate & Christy Johnston, R. Loren Sandford, Adam F. Thompson, Rebecca Greenwood, Rich Vera, Germaine Copeland, Jane Hamon, Tim Sheets, and Fiorella Giordano

## Compiled by Larry Sparks

DESTINY IMAGE® PUBLISHERS, INC.
P.O. Box 310, Shippensburg, PA 17257-0310
*"Promoting Inspired Lives."*

This book and all other Destiny Image and Destiny Image Fiction books are available at Christian bookstores and distributors worldwide.

Cover design by Eileen Rockwell
Interior design by Terry Clifton

For more information on foreign distributors, call 717-532-3040.
Reach us on the Internet: www.destinyimage.com.

ISBN 13 TP: 978-0-7684-4639-5
ISBN 13 eBook: 978-0-7684-4640-1
ISBN 13 HC: 978-0-7684-4642-5
ISBN 13 LP: 978-0-7684-4641-8

For Worldwide Distribution, Printed in the U.S.A.

3 4 5 6 7 8 / 23 22 21 20 19

# CONTENTS

# INTRODUCTION

RECENTLY, THE HOLY SPIRIT GAVE ME A VERY SIMPLE STATE-ment that is a fitting introduction for a compilation of prophetic words: "The prophets will prophesy." This sounds like a no-brainer, but in fact, I found it to be quite profound and revelatory. This one statement showed me how the prophetic operates and how God desires to see prophecies translate into realities.

This compilation of prophetic words is meant to provoke you to action, be it intercessory action or practical, boots-to-the-ground activism. It's not meant to simply inspire or encourage, although it will. Prophecies concerning times and seasons are meant to call the body of Christ into new realms of prayer, intercession, renewed thinking, wineskin adjustment, and Kingdom activity. Recently, the Lord specifically gave me two words—reorientation and realignment. What does this mean? Faith without works is dead, according to James. So, if we truly believe a prophetic word is applicable for our lives, personally or corporately for the Body of

Christ at large or for our city or nation, we need to do something with the word. Prophetic words demand stewardship.

## What Do You Do with Unfulfilled Prophetic Words?

I sense that prophetic words are seeking a landing place in the earth. The most qualified landing places for prophetic words are those who will set their hearts to *doing* what the words are calling for.

Many believers who have followed prophets and prophetic words over the years deal with a sense of spiritual aggravation concerning the fact that there are many words we have *yet* to see come to pass. They get frustrated because year after year, they feel like they heard the same words, over and over again. Sure, the prophecies might use different language from season to season, but overall, the words sound the same and they are accompanied by a nagging sense of unfulfillment. The aggravation is legitimate, but I don't believe it's aimed correctly. I sense the Spirit of the Lord is telling us to appropriately leverage the aggravation caused by unfulfilled words. May we be aggravated to take Kingdom action, not rest in spiritual complacency!

The prophets will keep prophesying the same thing, year after year, until these prophecies are fulfilled. Remember, that's what prophets will do; they are operating in their fivefold function as they prophesy! But maybe we are not seeing more corporate prophecies fulfilled because instead of participating with the prophetic words, we are waiting for the Sovereign God to bring something to pass that He didn't promise would happen by default.

## How Does the Prophetic Operate?

Let me provide you a quick view of how prophetic words operate. God, I believe, sovereignly distributes prophetic words to either prophets or believers who are operating in the gift of prophecy. God sovereignly gives words, previews, visions, dreams—supernatural snapshots, if you will—of His intended destiny for a person, community, nation, church, etc. God delivers these prophetic words in His way to His messengers in His time, and those messengers cannot help but prophesy the word of the Lord as they are gripped with what the Holy Spirit is saying. *"The Lord God has spoken! Who can but prophesy?"* (Amos 3:8). Hence, the prophets will continue to prophesy!

God sovereignly releases prophetic words from heaven, and prophets or prophetic people serve as the messengers of these words in the earth realm. What is our responsibility as recipients of prophetic words?

I repeat, *"Realign and reorient!"* These are two words the Lord gave me recently that directly apply to how we are called to steward the prophetic. If it's a legitimate word from heaven, biblically accurate, represents the nature of God as displayed through the canon of Scripture, and resonates with the spirit of the recipient(s), then a prophetic word has become an assignment. We need to participate with the word if we want to see it come to pass. Prophetic words call us to think differently, live differently, and function differently. They call us to expand the wineskin or operating system of the church, they provoke us to break out of religious cycles, and they beckon us to pray prayers and contend for realities that are completely out of our boxes of natural human limitation. Prophetic words give us God's vantage point on something and call us to come into agreement with His will and purposes.

It's with great excitement that I present to you this compilation of prophetic words for 2019, the Hebrew year 5779. Each voice, although different, provides a unique spiritual perspective on the movement of God in the coming year and new Kingdom era that we are entering.

Read these words and be inspired. But refuse to let the experience end there. Remember, prophetic words are meant to provoke you to action!

# No More Delay!

*Larry Sparks*

I HAD ONE PART OF THIS PROPHETIC WORD COMPLETED, BUT IT was on October 6, 2018 I received the second and missing installment.

That morning, I woke up with a sense of great expectation from the Lord. During lunch, I couldn't shake the phrase, "No more delay!" This is a decree I have heard issued from many reputable, global prophetic leaders including Chuck Pierce, Dutch and Tim Sheets, Robert Henderson, and others. I sensed an urgency on this statement, with the Lord pushing me to *do* something about it. "Why me, Lord? These generals of the faith do a far better job at communicating this message than I do!" God didn't seem impressed with my feedback and, thus, He has not changed the topic.

Just remember two things for this word—October 6 (10/6) and the phrase "No more delay." I want to revisit that statement at the end of this prophetic word and provide supernatural confirmation to you that, I believe, affirms this is an authentic word of the Lord for right now!

## The Time Is *Now!*

First, the Lord led me to revisit a portion of Scripture that I had been wrestling with in recent months:

> *Thus says the Lord of hosts: These people say the time has not yet come to rebuild the house of the Lord* (Haggai 1:2 ESV).

This prophetic oracle is intended for a very specific context—the "these people" of Haggai's day in regard to building God's house, the Temple. But I think we could easily see ourselves and our present generation in "these people." Today, we say things like "It's not time yet for global outpouring," or "It's not God's dispensation yet for revival," or "We're just waiting on God to pour out His Spirit when He wants." Heaven is ready while God's agents on earth seem to be delaying things. The problem is that we have embraced a theology that identifies God's sovereignty as the source of delay—I call this a theology of delay. While God does operate in times and seasons, there are certain things that heaven is waiting on earth for. For example, heaven is waiting on earth to steward the outpouring of Pentecost.

God sovereignly poured out His Spirit two thousand years ago in hopes that His ambassadors on earth, you and I, would actually steward His divine presence well and ultimately bring history into alignment with His Kingdom purposes. It goes without saying that we are seeing delay when it comes to seeing society and culture, let alone the Church, functioning in greater measures of God's glorious and righteous purposes.

Sadly, delay is often the result of delayed obedience to what God has called us to build. We are not focusing on what He is focused on (the outpouring of the Spirit on all flesh); therefore, we assume, using natural wisdom and logic, of course, that God wants us to build "buildings." Not simply church buildings, but more so, build natural things with Christian labels as opposed to building Him a place to dwell right in the middle of the gates of hell. The Lord actually desires a dwelling place positioned at the gates of hell—they pose no threat at all to Him. If anything, the presence of a people filled with His presence should pose a threat to the gates of hell. Jesus announced this when defining the purpose of His Ekklesia (see Matt. 16), and this assignment remains relevant to this very day.

## TAKE YOUR SEAT! DISPLACE AND OCCUPY

One thing that will immediately break delay in God's purposes being done in the earth will be the Spirit-filled community proactively stepping into spheres of society that have seats for Kingdom influence. Originally, I used the phrase "open seats," but the Spirit corrected me. Most of the "gates of influence" in the earth have seats, but they are not opened. The ones occupying seats of influence in the spirit world need to be displaced by an advancing, imposing Ekklesia. I am not speaking of a natural overthrowing; I am speaking of a people, called and assigned to occupy these seats, displacing powers of darkness and then claiming these seats of influence for the Kingdom. It's time! Either the seats are opened, or, more often than not, they are occupied by forces of darkness. It's time to displace darkness and establish Kingdom!

## WHY IS THERE DELAY FOR THE PURPOSES OF GOD?

I want to present to you some ways that the Holy Spirit informed me we are perpetuating delay when it comes to the purposes of God being fulfilled in the earth:

- **We simply don't ask**. *"You do not have because you do not ask"* (James 4:2 NKJV).

- **We pray "prayers" infected with doubt.** *"But when you ask him, be sure that your faith is in God alone. Do not waver, for a person with divided loyalty is as unsettled as a wave of the sea that is blown and tossed by the wind"* (James 1:6 NLT).

- **We've created a theology for delay.** When prayer is not answered, instead of contending with greater fervency or asking God for instruction, we settle into a theology that embraces delay as God's sovereign will.

- **Delayed obedience:** When we don't *do* what God directs, we will experience delay.

- **We are focusing on building things that God is not focused on—things He has not asked us to build.** This is exemplified in Haggai 1, where God's people were engaged in other building projects beside what God wanted to build in the earth.

- **Old wineskins and structures:** We are unwilling to accommodate the "new" move of the Spirit by allowing Him to interrupt what we are doing.

I'm convinced that for every source of delay, there is a *do*—something that the Body of Christ can do or execute—that can break or reverse delay. Start asking for things in prayer! Don't pray prayers infected with doubt but infused with faith! Refuse to partner with a theology of delay when you don't see immediate, instant results. Do what God says right when He asks you to do it! Build what God is calling you to build, not what you think makes sense or what contemporary Christianity applauds as "God's building project." Finally, be flexible to the outpouring of the Spirit—create an interruptible wineskin or infrastructure for God to move on His terms, in His way. Right here, I have provided redemptive solutions that will empower us to break delay!

## Two Prophetic Sources That Contribute to Delay

The Lord showed me two sources of reversible frustration in the Body of Christ concerning delay—unfulfilled personal prophetic words and unfulfilled corporate words to the Body of Christ. I repeat, these are reversible as I'm convinced the Lord has redemptive solutions for each source of frustration and aggravation.

### Delay of personal prophecy and prophetic words—no more "putting them on the shelf."

On a micro, individual level, we need to analyze "delay" when it comes to personal prophetic words. We have created an inappropriate doctrine in the Charismatic church that licenses us to put a prophetic word on the shelf when it seems like the timing is off for the word. It was the "right word, wrong time." There is some truth to this, of course. God operates in times and seasons. There are words whose fulfillment is reserved for a particular season in our lives, mainly because we need to undergo God's process to prepare us to carry the weight of prophetic fulfillment. I endorse process; I reject putting prophetic words on some kind of spiritual shelf.

Consider what happens as we receive prophetic words. We received something that resonated with our spirit, made us come to life, and called us into a new vision of destiny. What happened? We embraced a theology of delay. In this case, we attempted to wrap our natural mind around "how" this prophetic word would come to pass. Because the magnitude of the word seemed incompatible with our present situation or circumstance, we assumed the most logical thing to do was "put the word on a shelf." In other words, out of sight, out of mind until God sovereignly brings it back into focus or into fulfillment.

Yes, God the Sovereign King *can* certainly do that. But recently, in one of the few, very clear and vivid prophetic vision experiences I've had in my life, I saw a library in heaven. This library was filled with beautiful books, old and dusty. It was like the library in *Beauty and the Beast*. It was stunning, yet heartbreaking as I became aware of how much was stored up in heaven that was meant to find release and manifestation in the earth. I realized these books represented unfulfilled prophetic words that had been gathering dust because we embraced a theology of shelving the word of the Lord. There is a sobriety here that should strike us. And yet, the next scene revealed the extravagant mercy of the Lord. I saw the wind of God blow through the library. Dust started blowing off the tops of the books and the pages began flapping open in the wind. God the Sovereign was changing the times and seasons in the spirit. Even though God, in His sovereignty, is the One who delivers a prophetic word to us (through a prophet or prophetic person), we have a responsibility to respond and participate. The reason we are seeing so much delay is simple—we have not reoriented and recalibrated our lives to accommodate these prophetic words. God is so good, though! He is personally intervening, and with the breath of His Spirit He is blowing those pages open. This is a summons to you—revisit and review those words! Don't put them on a shelf in the spirit realm; hold them close to your heart.

I see the fear of the Lord returning to the delivery of personal prophecy. God, the One seated outside of time and above created order, sovereignly decides to release a sneak preview of His desired future from heaven into the earth through a prophetic vessel. The weight of this should fill us with awe! God delivers these sneak previews of the future through prophets and prophetic vessels—*to* us! Such words compel us to come into alignment with God's purpose and destiny for our lives. The problem? Often these words sound bigger than life. Rather than process them with God or pray through them or hold them close so we can wrestle with them, we embrace the theology of delay by placing them on a proverbial shelf. We hide them from view. What's really happening is God gave us these amazing gifts, prophetic words, and rather than holding them close, working with the Holy Spirit to discern, decipher, and execute on them, we send them back to heaven by shelving them. And the Lord says, "I don't want these books in heaven; I want these pages to become realities in the earth!"

I sensed an urgency in the spirit to decree that *now is the time! The wind of God is blowing the dust off the books.* It's a summons to the people of God to revisit personal prophetic words and promises from the Lord, and to hold them near. Keep them close. Yes, there are words that will find manifestation and fulfillment in a certain time; the problem is we can seem to postpone fulfillment, not because the delay was God-willed; rather, our lack of movement and response produced delay. This is not meant to condemn; it's called to provoke. I sense the Lord calling you to revisit past prophetic words expecting to be spiritually provoked and, yes, even experience a measure of "holy aggravation" over words that have not yet been fulfilled.

I believe the Lord is saying, "Leverage your aggravation correctly!" Again, many have been aggravated over unfulfilled prophetic words, and as a result they've rejected them completely or put them on the shelf. There is a holy aggravation that we are meant to live with, actually, that continually provokes us to contend for the fulfillment of God's promises. Let lack of fulfillment provoke you to cry out, ask, seek, knock, and converse with God *until* you see transformation.

## Delay of corporate prophecy and prophetic words coming to pass.

The Lord also took me through a process that I believe is meant to be healing for everyone who has been frustrated over corporate prophetic words that have not yet come to pass. I think of the globally recognized prophetic voices who are continually prophesying words of acceleration, awakening, glory, and breakthrough—and while it seems like the language may change, year after year, overall the realities that these prophets are announcing are the same and have not yet come to pass. This is a just cause for frustration in the Body of Christ. The problem is that much of our animosity gets aimed toward the prophets instead of the delay. We need to let it go and translate it into "holy aggravation." Leverage your spiritual aggravation; just don't aim it at the prophets, prophetic words, or even the Lord. Aim it at the delay, as it will provoke you to intercede and seek the Lord for executable strategy so that the words can translate from prophecy into manifestation.

The Lord told me, "Prophets will prophesy." Not very deep, but profound nonetheless. In other words, prophets will continue to prophesy—and often, prophesy the same things—because that is who they are and that is what they do. If the words don't come to pass, they will continue to declare them faithfully. As they continue to hear the word of the Lord, their voices will continue to roar its decree. Unfulfilled corporate prophecy in our churches, cities, regions, nations, and so forth should provoke and aggravate us, but we shouldn't aim these negative feelings at the prophets. No, aim your aggravation at the delay and commit to *do* something about it.

Prophecies demand action—participation. Delay will be broken when we decide to *do*. We need to execute apostolic strategies to partner with prophetic words. We need to adjust our mindsets and wineskins to accommodate the realms of glory, breakthrough, and acceleration that God desires to bring His people into. We need to readjust and realign our lives to accommodate the words that are being declared over us, if, in fact, we are expecting to see prophetic words come to fruition.

## THE *DO* OF REFORMATION WILL BREAK THE DELAY

The Lord is raising up a people who will break delay by doing what they have been called and assigned to do. Pretty simple. Reformation will be provoked by a people who encounter and do, who pray and do, who engage the spirit realm and do. We don't *do* something, or work, to gain God's favor. Quite the contrary. God in His mercy gave us prophetic words and Kingdom assignments to accomplish. We are called and assigned. We are not working to gain God's favor in order to receive an assignment; we've already been assigned. We simply need to follow through on what we have been called to do.

I see a convergence coming in the Body of Christ of three realms of function—prophet, priest, and governor, all pictured in Haggai 1. This convergence has the power to break the delays we are seeing, as it brings prophetic words, ministry leaders, and those called to the Seven Mountains into a dynamic reformational alliance. We will explore this further down the line, but it will be this threefold alignment operating in cooperation and harmony that will translate Holy Spirit renewal and revival into societal reformation.

I will share about this at the end of this compilation, as I provide the second part of the prophetic word I received for the coming season.

# 2019: "The Year of My Outstretched Arm and Major Demonstrations of My Power"

*Lana Vawser*

As we were about to move into 2018, the Lord spoke to me that 2018 was a year of "family, fruitfulness, and the fear of God"—that as the Church we are in a season of major restoration of the fear of God and Isaiah 6 encounters. That was a decree the Lord released in 2018 and that is now going to gain even greater momentum among the many other amazing things He is going to do in 2019.

The Lord has been moving in 2018. We as the Church are beginning to see the Lord show up in greater ways than ever before. He is leaving many in awe and wonder of Him. In 2019 and beyond, we are going to see Him move in ways that completely revolutionize the Church with dramatic demonstrations of His power and strength—a greater unveiling of His majesty!

About a month ago I heard the Lord release a decree over 2019. I heard Him say, "2019—the year of My outstretched arm and major demonstrations of My power."

I have such a deep stirring in my spirit as I sit with the Lord regarding 2019. He has been speaking to me that 2019 is going to be a year where the majesty of God is going to be revealed. We are truly going to see the Lord step in as the King of Kings and Lord of Lords.

There will be a great shaking, but it is a glorious shaking as the King of Glory truly steps in, in greater ways than we have ever seen. The Lord spoke to me over 18 months ago and told me that Psalm 24 is the decree over this time in history right now.

> So wake up, you living gateways! Lift up your heads, you ageless doors of destiny! Welcome the King of Glory, for he is about to come through you. You ask, "Who is this Glory-King?" The Lord, armed and ready for battle, the Mighty One, invincible in every way! So wake up, you living gateways, and rejoice! Fling wide, you ageless doors of destiny! Here he comes; the King of Glory is ready to come in (Psalm 24:7-9 TPT).

As I heard the Lord speak this, He reminded me of a dream I had many months before. In it, I heard His voice booming so loudly, it felt like the whole earth shook. He spoke: "Lana, it is not the end of a season; it is the end of an *era*. A completely new *era* has begun."

I woke up shaken by the voice and power of God. I knew we were in a major historical shift. In 2019 we are going to see mighty demonstrations of His power. We are going to see the outstretched arm of the Lord move in ways we have never seen. There are going to be mighty deliverances; there are going to be mighty demonstrations of the power of God that leave the Body of Christ and the earth shaken.

## IT IS A YEAR OF AWE

As I sat with the Lord talking with Him about 2019, He spoke "Lana, 2019—it is a year of awe." The Lord has been speaking for so long about the restoration of the fear of God in the Church. That is going to increase in 2019 and be seen in significant ways.

Many have been crying out to God, wondering why they do not yet have a "plan" or "strategy" for 2019. I want to encourage you—what the Lord is going to do in 2019 is going to be completely different. It is going to be a year when the Lord is going to take the Church and the world by surprise. I could hear His decree resonating: "2019, the year of being surprised by My power. You have no grid for what I am about to do; it's completely new" (see Isa. 43:19).

The way His power is going to manifest and His power be demonstrated, the testimony will be released far and wide across the world that He is the King of Kings and the Lord of Lords and He cannot be moved. He cannot be overcome. He cannot be shaken.

He spoke again:

"The earth will shake at My power and My decree in 2019. My majesty and holiness that is going to be revealed is going to leave the earth trembling—trembling at My power, My goodness, and My majesty. I am the King of Glory and I am coming in. I have been preparing My Church for such a time as this.

I am coming to reintroduce Myself to the Church and to the world. Where there has been familiarity that has been birthed in the Church, it is going to be shaken and broken in 2019. For I am restoring *awe* of who I am to the Church and to the world. I am going to cause the Church and the earth to *tremble* at My power. There are going to be so many 'face down' times in the Body of Christ and in the world in 2019 as I move in power. I am breaking boxes; I am breaking lies that have built themselves up against the truth of who I am. As My power is demonstrated; as governments are shaken, shifted, and moved; as things that would seem impossible will suddenly be accomplished in a day by My mighty power, My goodness is going to be revealed in My power that is going to bring in a mighty harvest. It is time for the great outpouring. It is time for My glory to be revealed. It is time not only for the Church to see My power and My glory, My majesty revealed, it is time for the earth to see My power and majesty in a way that has not been seen before."

## The Church Is Going to Tremble Again

"The Church is going to tremble again at My power and majesty."

There will be many times in 2019 that we as the people of God will be left trembling in His presence at the demonstration of His power and majesty. The fear of God is being restored—an awe at the holiness of God. From that place will arise an army that is carrying and moving in the power of God in ways we have never seen before.

The great trembling is going to bring forth a great *maturity*. It is going to bring forth a *maturing* of the saints to carry His glory and to see His power flow through them like never before. It's birthing a *purity* and an *integrity* in the people of God to reflect Him in brighter ways than before.

The fear of God in the Church is going to shake out and clean out impurities and strengthen God's people to partner with Him in the greatest move of the Spirit of God upon the Church that we have ever seen.

> *The entire universe is standing on tiptoe, yearning to see the unveiling of God's glorious sons and daughters!* (Romans 8:19 TPT)

## THE YEAR OF MY OUTSTRETCHED ARM

There are going to be mighty demonstrations of deliverance in 2019. The Lord is going to bring a mighty deliverance to the Body of Christ and to the earth. There is a mighty refiner's fire that is going to increase in 2019 in the Church, but it is not something to run away from—it's something to *run toward*. For the purifying fire of God is bringing great deliverance. His strong arm is coming to deliver His people from their bondage. In this new era we will see a mighty demonstration of the freedom of God in the Church. The saints of God have been held down too long. The saints of God have been caged in lies and fears and bondages that have already been dealt with at the cross by Jesus, and it is *time* for the saints to go free.

Get ready to see mighty, mighty, mighty deliverances take place in 2019. The Lord is going to show Himself strong to deliver His people from their captivity see (Ps. 136:12-14).

I heard the Lord say again: "I am going to remind you again! I am going to remind you again of what is yours and *who I am*."

As He spoke those words, I had a vision. I saw Jesus on the cross and then the Lord rising out of the tomb in resurrection power. The atmosphere was filled with victory and triumph. He spoke again:

"I am going to remind My people again of their victory in Me. I am going to reveal Myself in powerful ways as the King of Kings, the Lord of Victory, the God of breakthrough, the Warrior God. I am going to remind My people again of their victory. Where they have forgotten, I am going to remind them again who I am and who they are in Me. The mighty demonstrations of My power are going to *suddenly shake My people awake* in new ways. My people have begun to wake, but there is going to be a glorious, violent shaking awake by My power that is going to leave My people in awe of who I am.

"The world is going to see My mighty deliverance, My mighty power and strength, My outstretched arm to deliver and rearrange and sovereignly establish My plans upon the earth in 2019. My mighty arm will be showed strong. I have been known as the Lamb; now I shall be known as the *Lion*! I am going to *roar in strength* in the earth like never before in 2019."

## A Great Awakening

*I can do all things through Christ who strengthens me* (Philippians 4:13 NKJV).

*Looking straight into their eyes, Jesus replied, "Humanly speaking, no one, because no one can save himself. But what seems impossible to you is never impossible to God!"* (Matthew 19:26 TPT)

In 2019, the power of God is going to usher in a mighty awakening of Philippians 4:13 and Matthew 19:26. This will be demonstrated in the lives of His people individually, in the Body of Christ, and in the earth.

It is going to ignite the fire in the Body of Christ that all things are possible in Christ. In 2019, many things that seem "impossible" will be suddenly overturned by the power of God. Mighty, loud demonstrations of His power will raise up an army of God, moving in the resurrection power of God.

Mighty miracles of the resurrection power of God will suddenly take place. I heard the Lord decreeing over and over: "2019—a year of My *resurrection power!*"

The power of His resurrection will *rebirth many* in the Body of Christ. There will be *many* powerful moves of the Spirit of God that will bring forth *mighty* resurrection power in the Church.

> *I pray that you will continually experience the immeasurable greatness of God's power made available to you through faith. Then your lives will be an advertisement of this immense power as it works through you! This is the mighty power that was released when God raised Christ from the dead and exalted him to the place of highest honor and supreme authority in the heavenly realm!* (Ephesians 1:19-20 TPT)

In 2019, this divine rebirthing will see the Spirit of God raise up His army that moves in His resurrection power. I see the army of God moving out into the world—no longer chained by fear but convicted by the power and protection of God and moving forward face to face with impossibilities and giants and decreeing, "*Nothing is impossible for Him! He lives in me! Impossibilities bow!*"

There will also be many demonstrations of the resurrection power of Jesus in the world in 2019 and beyond. The dead will be raised more and more. God is about to show up *mightily* in power and the world *will* take notice. A *mighty increase* of harvest, an influx of souls into the Kingdom of God will take place as they physically *see* the resurrection power of God demonstrated before their very eyes.

The Lord showed me where the enemy has fought *so hard* in the last few years to kill dreams, assignments, and people in the Body of Christ in an attempt to take them out. Now 2019 will see a *divine rebirth* of God's people that will move them further into their destiny and purpose. The God of *breakthrough* is upon us, and the resurrection power of God is going to bring a great *overturning* of the dead and dry places.

## Esther Season: Accelerated Positioning and Repositioning

This is an Esther season right now, and this divine rebirth that is going to take place is going to raise up God's people into a greater level of positioning to release His love, His goodness, and His power in the earth. There is going to be *accelerated promotion* and *positioning* in 2019. There will be many *sudden positionings* and *repositionings* in 2019 in both the Church and the world. I saw in a vision the hand of the Lord repositioning pieces on a chessboard at an accelerated pace. As He was moving, shifting, rearranging, and repositioning, I heard the sounds of "grumbling" in the Body of Christ.

The sound of grumbling rose from the Church: "They shouldn't be there," "I don't agree with that positioning," "They are not right for that position." I heard the Lord release a warning for 2019.

In the mighty positioning and repositioning of God in 2019 I heard Him say, "Do *not* despise the positioning. Continue to ask for eye salve to *see* what I am doing. For My positioning is perfect. Do not speak *poison* over My positioning. You *must* lean in, in 2019 more than ever, to have My heart, to know My Word, and to hear My voice. Continue to ask for eye salve in 2019 to *discern* the new thing I am doing. For there will be many surprises in the positioning, but My positioning is *perfect*."

## THERE WILL BE A "CROSSROAD CHOICE"

The Lord showed me there is going to be a "crossroad choice" for many in 2019. People will reach the place that says, "Do I go the way I think I should go or the way God is going?" For the pathways the Lord is going to lead His people upon in 2019, for some, may feel "off the beaten track." For many it will be very uncomfortable—a place they have never been before. But these pathways that seem so "out of left field" and so completely "not what I expected" are going to be the places of greater destiny, greater life and positioning to see His power move through them in ways they have never seen.

There will be *many* times in 2019 when people will find themselves completely out of their comfort zones and in a place that feels like it surpasses their capacity. That's the point. The Lord is going to demonstrate His power *so profoundly through you* in 2019, it is going to cause a beautiful, deeper level of intimacy with Jesus in your life. You will *see Him* move through you in ways you could never accomplish yourself. It's a glorious place.

But there will be a temptation in these uncomfortable places to stay in what you have known or what you "want." I want to encourage you that the plans and pathways of God are *far better* than what you have dreamt for yourself.

These crossroad choices in 2019 will birth in you a resolve that no one will ever take from you if you choose *His way*. It will build a fortification in you that will never be stolen. It will see you positioned for a greater impartation of His fire to say, "*I will go wherever You lead me.*" It's a greater and louder *yes* to Him to follow Jesus. A deeper level of radical abandonment to Him and His calling. A fire that burns only to see His name lifted high, His glory and goodness seen across the earth, and a place of awakening to the privilege that it is to represent Jesus and the gospel in the earth.

In these "crossroad choice" places, the place of deeper *yes* given to the Lord, there will be an even greater increase that will be released upon the Church. We cannot even begin to imagine the increase God is getting ready to release in 2019, but this increase *must* be carried by a heart that is laid down and living for *Him* and *His way*, moving in maturity and not living in soulish agenda but pure devotion to their first love—*Jesus!*

## A Roar of My Justice

"As my power and majesty is demonstrated in the Church and across the earth in exponential ways in 2019, the roar of My justice will come forth! I will roar My justice over the Church that will bring sudden shifts, sudden breakthroughs, and sudden restorations, but I will also roar My justice over the nations.

"I decree that in 2019, the nations will tremble at the *roar of My justice* and My power and *every knee* will bow and *every tongue* will confess that I am Lord. I am revealing My justice and overturning the injustice that has taken place for so long. There will be a mighty acceleration seen in the earth in 2019— My *justice* overturning injustice. There will be mighty demonstrations that I am the God who sits in the heavens and laughs at the plans of man. I am going to move *mightily* in power. I will demonstrate My power that I am the God who cannot be moved. I will shake and I will rearrange to bring forth *My glory*. To bring forth the greatest time upon the earth of My glory being seen. It's time for *more*! It's time for the nations to *see* that I am the Lord. My kindness and My power will bring forth a *mighty* repentance in the earth and the nations will begin to *shake* and change. Yes, there will be significant uproars and battles, but My people *must* remember that My roar of justice is being released upon the earth and the *roar of My victory* is being released. *My roar is opening up the gates of victory!* The gates of *victory* are now being opened. The shaking must come through the roar of My justice to bring forth My *victory* and usher in My glory. Truly I am bringing My people to the place of faith that *believes* with great fire and conviction that a *nation can be* changed in a day. The *roar* of My justice over the nations will activate a great *birthing* in the nations to see My Kingdom and glory come and My name lifted high.

"Don't be afraid when you see the nations shake. *Know* that the roar of My victory and justice is being released!"

## Marked By My Majesty

I heard the Lord say, "Get ready, My people. Get ready in 2019 to be *marked by My majesty!*"

I saw such a branding taking place upon the people in 2019 by the *majesty* of God being revealed in the Church. Marked for life and forever changed by the revelation of His majesty, who He is, and His power. It's going to change everything. The Body of Christ and the world will never be the same. As the King of Glory steps in, things will not be the same. Don't try and hold on to what has been, don't try to work things out in your head, just look for Him and trust Him.

A great unveiling is about to take place—King of Glory, King of Majesty, come in!

# About Lana Vawser

Lana Vawser is first and foremost, a pursuer of God's heart and secondly, a prophetic voice to the nations. Her desire is to help people develop deep intimacy with Jesus and activate their prophetic hearing to recognize God speaking in everyday life. Lana is driven by a vision to see people set free and walking in the abundant life that Jesus purchased for them. She is an itinerant preacher and prophetic revivalist who gets to participate in powerful moves of God throughout the nations. Lana is married to Kevin and they live in Brisbane, Australia, with their two sons.

# A Year Marked by the Holy Ghost, Holiness, and New Wine

*Nate Johnston*

Sons and daughters of God live for revival. It's in our DNA to see God manifest Himself in all of His glory to a world craving His touch, and I believe we are right now poised and positioned for the greatest impact and exploits that will fill the pages of history. The word you are about to read is an invitation, a branding, a deep marking of fire to those who are hungry to be used by God in the year ahead and see Jesus get His full reward!

## The Wrestle of the Season

As I was asking the Lord what He was speaking over the year, He highlighted both the number 9, from the Jewish calendar year 5779 we are currently in, and 19. The following are the prophetic keys for the year 2019, which God spoke to me through these two numbers.

### 9

The ninth letter of the Jewish alphabet is *tet,* which is a letter of double meaning with the symbol of the womb/vessel/basin, or also seen as the snake in the basket. Tet is first used in Genesis in creation and speaks of bringing forth goodness. It is the birthing of the new with God, just as there are nine months in a pregnancy. When I was asking Holy Spirit about it, I heard the scripture from Acts 2:4: ***"All of them were filled with the Holy Spirit and began to speak in other tongues as the Spirit enabled them"*** (NIV). So this letter to me speaks of the fresh infilling of the Holy Ghost in this season.

The number nine also represents the nine fruits of the Spirit and the nine gifts of the Spirit. Many have been feeling dry and empty, and God is saying that this year there is a fresh invitation to be filled by His Spirit that will usher in a mighty move of His Spirit that will touch the nations. The snake in the basket represents refusing to move with the Holy Spirit and living in our own strength and ability. In the Garden of Eden Adam and Eve chose to be tempted by the snake to eat the wrong fruit. We have the choice to either conceive with the Holy Spirit and give birth to the fruit He wants us to have or to be fruitless. The snake also represents the exposing of the enemy's plans personally and in the nations in this season. This to me speaks highly of hidden political agendas and injustices that have been swept under the carpet.

### 19

The 19th letter of the Hebrew alphabet is *kuf,* which like tet is another letter with a double meaning of good and bad. It means both "holiness" and "shells/husks," which denotes both purity and cleanliness and also the chaff that the fire of God extinguishes—which ironically produces holiness. What struck me about this letter is that it is the only letter that descends below the line in the whole Hebrew alphabet. It uses the letter *zayin*—the symbol of the sword, which speaks of the cutting and purifying process that results in holiness. The top stroke of the letter is formed from the Hebrew letter *reish*, which means "head." To me this speaks yet again of the wrestle between our human minds and the Spirit of God.

## The Fire before the Wave

Recently I was in worship when I saw a vision of waters receding on a beach, moving back at a rapid rate out into the sea. As it moved I could see all the shells, stones, and seaweed that were sitting on the ocean floor. Then the wind began to howl loudly around me and I could see in the far distance a huge wave that was cresting and about to make impact. I knew this was a mighty unleashing of the Holy Spirit upon the earth. The receding waters exposed what was on the bottom of the ocean. The Lord told me that we are in a season when He is correcting and aligning foundations that have been cracked and are in disrepair so we 1) know how to ride the wave, and 2) can sustain the move of God. The recession of the water also represented the season of exposing the enemy's plans and assignments to distract and delay the purposes and plans of God.

> *He will sit as a refiner and purifier of silver; he will purify the Levites and refine them like gold and silver. Then the Lord will have men who will bring offerings in righteousness* (Malachi 3:3 NIV).

God is refining us as we cross over, healing us, and realigning us because many have been in holding patterns—delayed, stunted, and stuck in dysfunctional cycles, never beholding their promised land, unable to bring forth what God has placed inside them. This will be a year that the Body of Christ will experience the bondage-crushing break-through anointing of the Holy Spirit. It will remove long-standing obstacles that have been shackling them for years so they can participate in and propagate the outpouring of God's Spirit on the earth.

## Breaking the Mold

I was in worship about to step up to speak earlier in the year when I felt the tangible glory of God rest upon me heavily and I could barely stand. As I sat down on my chair to make sense of what God was doing, He spoke something loud and clear: "Will you move out of the way?"

My instant response was, "Yes, Lord, of course!" As I got up to speak I still felt the weight of His presence and had zero ability to take control, so I just allowed Holy Spirit to do what He was wanting to do. Over the hour that followed the Holy Spirit moved in an unusual way. I even lay down on the stage at one point! That meeting was a point of no return for me. When we are fully yielded to the Spirit, God's glory is fully unveiled to the world, and I believe this year the Holy Spirit wants to unveil Jesus the King of Glory to the world through completely yielded vessels.

> *The entire universe is standing on tiptoe, yearning to see the unveiling of God's glorious sons and daughters!* (Romans 8:19 TPT)

There is something about laying down the old in this season that will result in God *birthing* the new! The invitation in this coming year is to simply partner with Him by laying down our ways and methods and step out of the way so He can move how He wants to.

## The New Wine

As we crossed over into the Jewish year 5779 we were in another city speaking at a conference. The night before, I dreamt of the region we were staying in being flooded by wine, but what I saw was that this wine was sinking deep into the earth and, like a flood, began exposing what lay underneath. This wine was healing and redemptive, and it was realigning the destiny of the region, which was actually a wincry region!

When Jesus turned the water into wine at the wedding in Cana it was a prophetic act of the changing of an era. In the same way right now God is pouring out new wine because we are stepping into a new *era* where we will need the new wine to see the great harvest come flooding in. Jesus made the clear distinction at the Cana wedding that if He produced wine, *it would change everything!* He knew that this simple act was more than just satisfying the wedding guests' thirst, but it prophetically spoke of the new wine that would be Pentecost. Under Jesus' direction, the servers filled up six water pots with water that were used for purification. Six is the number of man and speaks of the limitations of man's ability, but when God fills us we become pure and then flow with new wine that is better than the old batch!

> *And he gave them this illustration: "No one rips up a new garment to make patches for an old, worn-out one. If you tear up the new to make a patch for the old, it will not match the old garment. And who pours new wine into an old wineskin? If someone did, the old wineskin would burst and the new wine would be lost. New wine must always be poured into new wineskins. Yet you say, 'The old ways are better,' and you refuse to even taste the new that I bring"* (Luke 5:36-39 TPT).

The new cloth will always reveal the weakness of the old cloth, and the new wine will always cause the old wineskin to rupture. The Lord told me that the old wineskin in the Church would burst in 2019, and the Church will be faced with the choice between powerless religion or embracing the new wine and move of the Spirit.

## Choose the New Wine!

Have you experienced areas of your life that just aren't working like they used to? Are you suddenly not hearing God in the same way? Are doors that were opened suddenly closed to you? God may be trying to lead you in a way that will produce a greater result than you are used to. After Jesus died the disciples went back to their old professions because they still weren't filled with the Spirit and couldn't see the new era upon them. Jesus yelled out from the shore to cast their net on the other side, and as they did they pulled in more fish than they knew what to do with!

We have to adjust in this season. The old wine simply will not sustain you in this new season; in fact, it will only cause you to settle for the results and fruit of a past season. Often what carries new wine will also defy the current norms that are changing or transitioning, and you'll be faced with the decision to either *bow* and back down or push through the fear and embrace the fresh thing the Holy Spirit is doing.

As we crossed the threshold into 5779, I saw two arms in the spirit. One arm was the might and strength of the Holy Spirit, and the other was the arm of man—the strength and ability of man that is rising right now. I knew that these arms were clashing moves of two very different kingdoms. All throughout the Bible arms represent strength, battle, might, and power. The temptation is even greater to operate in the strength of self and to push forward in the driven pursuit of man, but choose the Spirit! We are going to see the firstfruits or contractions of labor of a move of God hit the nations, but it will take focus and discernment to bring it forth. It is opposed by the competitive agenda of man that wants to control, dominate, orchestrate, and order his own steps.

The new wine is gushing forth, and it isn't necessarily flowing in the way most will expect. Only those who follow His voice will see it. The fear of man will always want you to trade in your chips for cheap wine; religion will want you to police the flow, while the Holy Spirit is saying, "Jump in, jump in, jump in!" Even right now you can feel the uncomfortable tension as God is calling you to venture beyond the expected, and you may even feel dissatisfaction with the norm. Your womb is leaping, your passion is resurging, and you are longing to see the Lord move mightily upon your life. It's time for the *new wine!*

## The Year of Greatest Export

As the Holy Spirit reignites hearts, the Church will enter into new territory we have not even imagined we would possess. I heard the Lord say that 2019 is a year for nations to be won as the move of the Spirit erupts in the most unlikely of places and in the most unreached corners of the earth. I kept seeing embers of a fire flicking out of heaven's fiery furnace of this move and exporting sons and daughters into these nations as a stake in the ground. These sent ones will conceive in this hour and carry a cry for the nations to see them claimed for the Kingdom.

I believe this will be such a year of never-before-seen export to the nations. The wine that has been produced in you through your season of pressing has produced His finest vintage yet, and you and I are in high demand to export heaven's goods to earth. This is a year for the Church to shine like never before and to reveal itself in purity and strength and be the remedy to a world in crisis. I prophesy that your 2019 will be a year of such powerful visitation and fresh infilling that you overflow everywhere you go, awakening homes, regions, cities, and nations to the gospel in Jesus' name!

# About Nate Johnston

Nate Johnston is a revivalist and worshiper who has a heart to see sons and daughters unleashed into passionate friendship with God and an effective supernatural lifestyle. Through his ministry, Everyday Revivalists, he teaches on intimacy and hearing God's voice which was birthed from a hunger for authentic, real, and powerful relationship with Jesus.

# THE ERA OF THE HOLY SPIRIT AND UNPRECEDENTED BIRTHING

*Christy Johnston*

THIS IS A TIME OF UNPRECEDENTED BIRTHING. AS I WAS PRAY-
ing with the Holy Spirit about this hour that we find ourselves in,
I saw a vision of an antique treasure chest hidden under my bed. In this
vision, I had no prior awareness of the existence of this treasure chest, and
it felt as though it had been concealed from my sight and secretly kept
until this moment. As I pulled out the dusty chest and opened it up, I

discovered inside it a myriad of aged pages, each of them inscribed with elegant handwritten calligraphy.

I began to draw out one tired page at a time and read their messages. The contents surprised me. One page after another contained dreams that I had conceived as a little child, a teenager, and even into my early adulthood years that had died in my heart out of disappointment or had been long forgotten. They were all there. Even though this was a vision, it moved me emotionally as the Holy Spirit brought to my memory the long-lost dreams of my heart, and I instinctively knew that it was He who had written them. Some of these dreams were what I would have considered insignificant in the context of eternity, but they were all there from the smallest to the largest. The Holy Spirit had penned every single one of my dreams and concealed them for this ordained moment. The vision concluded as the Holy Spirit spoke these words to my heart: "Now is the time to birth."

I believe in this coming year the Holy Spirit is resurrecting the long-lost and forgotten dreams of our hearts; He is breathing new life into what seemed impossible or the dreams we let go of from seasons of disappointment and pain. Birthing, though it is a time of great joy, is also often a time of immense pain, and in light of that thought I began to consider how this coming time of birthing is not just reserved for us individually but for the nations. I don't mean to say that we are going to further experience great pain, but rather, the events that have already transpired on a personal level and the global stage all point to the sounds of grueling labor. The earth has been groaning in anticipation of the birthing and awakening of God's sons and daughters.

The dreams that you lost or let go are the dreams that have been conceived in the heart of our Father, and they are a treasure to Him. The Holy Spirit is resurrecting these dreams in this moment because they carry strategies and blueprints for your life and the lives of those around you. He is activating the seed of your dreams, because when birthed they will unlock supernatural answers for the world that will pave the way for this generation to know Jesus.

While I recognize that we have already been witnessing the early signs of the great awakening, I believe this hour in history has been held for the unparalleled birthing of a new era that is now upon us. I don't believe this to be just another season, but rather a brand-new era. An era is defined as a long and distinct period of time. The dictionary also describes an era as the period of time to which anything belongs or is to be assigned. When I discovered that definition, the Spirit of God spoke to my heart, "This is My era; it has been assigned to Me." This epoch period of time belongs to and has been assigned to the Holy Spirit. It is the era of the Spirit of God. Whereas past eras have been defined by events, this moment of history will be defined by a worldwide birthing of sons and daughters into the Kingdom of God.

> *Who has heard of such a thing? Who has seen such things? Shall a land be born in one day? Or shall a nation be brought forth in a moment? For as soon as Zion was in labor, she brought forth her children* (Isaiah 66:8 AMPC).

## A Dream about Quintuplets

I recently had a dream that I knew was further confirmation of this era of birthing. In the dream, my husband Nate and I were inspecting a newly established hospital in the heart of China. Government officials were taking us on a tour through each delivery room as they were proudly displaying their state-of-the-art establishment and equipment. It was the first of its kind in China and it had just opened the day before. While we were in the middle of a large delivery room admiring all of its features, suddenly the doors burst open, and rushing through those doors were five midwives, each carrying a newborn baby. The midwives were ecstatic with delight, each of them either crying in joy uncontrollably or laughing and shouting.

It was quite the commotion, and it took us all by surprise. The midwives then placed all five babies in the arms of Nate and I—three were snuggled into my arms and Nate gently held the other two. The atmosphere of the room had very abruptly transformed into an electric celebration; however, I was still unaware of the profound significance of what was happening. The midwives began shouting in their local dialect, "This is unprecedented."

I was able to understand their language, and I responded with the question, "Why is this so remarkable?"

A government official turned to me and quietly whispered, "This has never happened before in the history of our country. These babies have all been born to the same mother; they are quintuplets." The mother of the quintuplets then entered the room looking happy, healthy, and full of wonder. I looked down at the faces of her precious newborns calmly asleep in my arms and marveled at the miracles I was holding. It was the kind of dream that stays with you for days.

Following this dream, I was in awe when a news article was sent to me regarding China. The article detailed at great length a sudden increased wave of severe persecution upon the church there. Given what I had just dreamt that night, it both grieved and intrigued me more than perhaps it had ever before. I believe this dream was both weighty for the country of China while simultaneously speaking for the nations.

China has long been known for its persecution of the church, and in very recent times this persecution has increased. This same spirit of persecution has also been multiplying in measure across the international arena, and I believe this dream and the current times of persecution aligned for a reason. Interestingly, China is also well known for its strict "family planning" regime, whereby the government permits parents to have only one or two children under the orders of their current two-child policy. I believe the quintuplets being born into this kind of regional climate points to this era of monumental birthing despite the opposition toward the church. This is indeed a time of unprecedented birthing. Regardless of the agendas of the enemy to stifle, withhold, silence, manipulate, and restrict the people of God, there will be an unstoppable movement of glory as His Spirit moves mightily and a momentous number of souls are birthed into the Kingdom of God.

The surprise of the five newborns in the dream, an event that had "never happened before," points again to this era of the Spirit—a time of bizarre and exceptional supernatural birthing unlike anything that has ever been seen before. The number five in Hebrew is symbolic of grace. The Holy Spirit led me to Isaiah 55:5, which decrees: *"Surely you will summon nations you know not, and nations you do not know will come running to you, because of the Lord your God, the Holy One of Israel, for he has endowed you with splendor"* (NIV). I strongly believe this is a time when the Holy Spirit is causing the Church to arise and summon the nations to Jesus. The earth's atmosphere is going to abruptly transform into celebration as the sounds of salvation erupt across every nation, and I believe we will witness governmental officials participating in the outpouring. Just as the midwives marveled in the dream, we will stand in awe and astonishment. Lastly, the healthy mother, I believe, denotes the healthy Bride.

## It's Time to Push!

I'll never forget when I birthed my second daughter and it came time for me to push. I felt elation that the end of my labor was in sight and soon I would hold my precious newborn, but I was simultaneously feeling an exhaustion I had never endured before. This feeling was overshadowing any joy on my horizon. I had been laboring through intense contractions for three whole days—more specifically, over 80 hours. I was weak from having little sleep and hardly any food while being in a constant state of pain. So when I was finally able to push, I had scarcely any energy to do so. I remember saying through tears, "I can't do this. I am in too much pain, I have no energy, and I can't go any further."

At that moment, my midwife got down at eye level with me and looked me square in the eyes. "Honey, you were born to do this, you are capable and strong. Now, let's get this done; it's time to *push*." Her words gave me the strength I needed to go on, and just 20 minutes later, Sophie was born.

I believe many have been weary from the long labors of a fight. Much like how I was at the end of myself from an excruciatingly long labor, your battles have been lengthier than anticipated and fiercer than you could have imagined. You have been saying, "I can't go on any further, I have nothing left in me to fight, I don't even know how to dream anymore." I believe the same can be said when we look at the tumult of the nations, and maybe you have been saying about your own nation, "It looks too difficult to ever imagine a move of God here."

I am here to remind you that the Holy Spirit is your midwife and He is coaching you through this birthing. He is right beside you as you navigate your way through labor. Can you hear Him? "Beloved, I know you're tired, I know you're exhausted, but now is not the time to give up. The promise is about to birth. It's time to *push!*" It is time to push on the promises of God for your life personally and for the nations.

It is noteworthy that the Hebrew number nine (for the Hebraic year of 5779 and the Gregorian year of 2019) is symbolic of both birthing and the Holy Spirit. He is the midwife and He is calling you forth to push on His promises until you see them birthed and fulfilled. He is inviting you and me to partner with Him to push on His promises for the nations. He is getting down with you at your eye level and reminding you that despite the difficulties you have faced, you can do this. It is His spoken word that infuses you with the courage and strength you need to see the dream birthed into fruition. He is reminding you and me of this very promise:

*"Shall I bring to the [moment of] birth and not cause to bring forth? says the Lord. Shall I Who causes to bring forth shut the womb? says your God"* (Isaiah 66:9 AMPC).

It is time to birth.

# ABOUT CHRISTY JOHNSTON

CHRISTY JOHNSTON WAS BORN AND RAISED IN AUSTRALIA. AFTER living the majority of her life plagued with insecurity and fear, she came to learn the power of her identity in Christ. She now lives with the mandate to breathe fresh hope and life into Gods sons and daughters through her passion of writing, uncovering the truths of living in Grace and freedom through our identity in Christ. Nate and Christy have two daughters, Charlotte and Sophie, and currently live in Brisbane Australia.

# The Process of the New Wine

*Robert Henderson*

On the third day there was a wedding in Cana of Galilee, and the mother of Jesus was there. Now both Jesus and His disciples were invited to the wedding. And when they ran out of wine, the mother of Jesus said to Him, "They have no wine." Jesus said to her, "Woman, what does your concern have to do with Me? My hour has not yet come." His mother said to the servants, "Whatever He says to you, do it." Now there were set there six waterpots of stone, according to the manner of purification of the Jews, containing twenty or thirty gallons apiece. Jesus said to them, "Fill the waterpots with water." And they filled them up to the brim. And He said to them, "Draw some out now, and take it to the master of the feast." And they took it. When the master of the feast had tasted the water that was made wine, and did not know where it came from (but the servants who had drawn the water knew), the master of the feast called the bridegroom. And he said to him, "Every man at the beginning sets out the good wine, and when the guests have well drunk, then the inferior. You have kept the good wine until now!" This beginning of signs Jesus did in Cana of Galilee, and manifested His glory; and His disciples believed in Him.

—John 2:1-11 NKJV

In this story I believe we have a prophetic word for 5779/2019. There is a release of glory, power, and new wine coming into the earth. The Lord is taking the tasteless, insipid, and odorless realms of our life and transforming them into life more abundantly. He is also taking that which the church has been offering to the world and changing it into that which is life-changing and culture shaping.

There are several things that were involved in this first miracle of Jesus. First, this miracle happened at a wedding. A wedding speaks of a place of covenant. Covenant is necessary for houses to be built. Houses are what the Lord uses to rule the earth. Among other places, in Isaiah 2:2 we see the importance of houses.

> Now it shall come to pass in the latter days that the mountain of the Lord's house shall be established on the top of the mountains, and shall be exalted above the hills; and all nations shall flow to it (NKJV).

The mountain of the Lord's house is established and ruling over all other mountains. This speaks of a governmental people who are allowing and disallowing things in the earth on a very high level. This is the Church/ecclesia. The problem is that these kinds of houses cannot be formed and functioning without covenant. People's lives coming together in covenant relationships that are unbreakable allow this level of authority to operate. In 5779/2019 there will be a new level of covenant that allows these kinds of houses to be built and operating. As a result of this, a governmental release of God's judicial order and justice will be seen in the nations.

Jesus' turning the water to wine also prophetically speaks to us that it is His heart for the party to continue. In the natural scheme of things, there was nothing earth-shaking hanging in the balance. A wedding festival might have ended prematurely without more wine. Perhaps you may have lost the zest for life. Maybe you no longer relish the beauty of living and loving life the way you once did. When Jesus turned the water to wine, He was voting for the party to continue. Jesus intends to bring the joy and zest of life back to His people and cause them to rejoice. Proverbs 15:15 tells us that when we have the joy of the Lord, we are in a continual party:

> *All the days of the afflicted are evil, but he who is of a merry heart has a continual feast* (NKJV).

There is coming in 5779/2019 a new dimension of joy and excitement in the Lord. Depression will wane, anxiety will diminish, and those afflicted by oppression will be freed. Jesus will turn the water into wine. There will be a societal outpouring of the Spirit of the Lord that not only will rival but will exceed the Charismatic Renewal and Jesus People Movement of the '60s and '70s. Whereas there has been only the water of religion and the seeker-sensitive movement, there will now be the power and glory of Jesus, the manifested Christ. The Spirit and Bride say come to the Bridegroom (see Rev. 22:17). There is a passion arising in the spirit realm causing a cry to come forth for the manifestation of His glory. The best wine of the Spirit of the Lord has now been saved for the last. In the mercy of the Lord, God will visit His people and inheritance again and the cultures of the earth will shake with His presence.

Another thing that is prophetically relevant in this story is Jesus at first refused to do anything about the shortage of wine. When, however, the servants showed a willingness to obey whatever He said, Jesus' attitude toward the situation changed. He went from clearly not feeling any level of responsibility in the matter to moving in faith to see water become wine. We must know that willingness and obedience move the heart of God. If we want the Lord to move and manifest His glory, it is a willingness and obedience in us that will draw this out of the Lord. We must repent anywhere we have exhibited a stubborn and self-willed heart and allow ourselves to be brought to brokenness and surrender. When we do, the glory and power of the Lord will be seen. I prophesy a new level of brokenness and repentance in the Church from the fear of the Lord. I declare that there will be humble broken people filled with the boldness of the Lord in 5779/2019.

The other thing I see for 5779/2019 is an increase of the hidden ones' function that gives birth to this which is being prophesied. It was the servants who knew *how* the miracle happened. All the rest only got the benefit of it. The servants, however, through their obedience *caused* it. There is a new passion arising in the hidden ones who, through their obedience in prayer, will see the water turned to wine.

The Master of the feast commented on the best wine being saved for last. However, it says the servants knew where it had come from. They knew the price of obedience they had paid to fill six containers that would hold 20 to 30 gallons apiece. They had the sweat on their brow, the blisters on their hands, the ache in their backs, and the exhaustion of their obedience testifying to the price of this miracle. Those who think the suddenlies of God happen without human effort or obedience are sadly mistaken. The suddenlies are not suddenlies to those who have caused them. They have a history of obedience with God in prayer, intercession, weeping, and travail that has moved things in the spirit world to allow everyone else to marvel at what has occurred.

God is coming in 5779/2019 to greatly empower the servants behind the scenes. He is placing much honor on the hidden ones who are producing what is necessary for the water to be made wine. Those who have been held in low or no esteem will have the honor of the Lord thrust upon them in this hour.

I also hear the Lord saying that He is coming to refresh the weary and the fatigued. The weak shall say I am strong. I hear Zechariah 12:8:

> *In that day the Lord will defend the inhabitants of Jerusalem; the one who is feeble among them in that day shall be like David, and the house of David shall be like God, like the Angel of the Lord before them* (NKJV).

God is coming with His defense for those who have been afflicted and attacked. Those who are feeble will become as David, the mighty warrior of God. Those who are as David will become like God, even like the Angel of the Lord who goes before us. I say to the weak, in 5779/2019 arise and step into your strength. For you will do exploits in the Name of the Lord! Your days and times of weakness and ridicule are over. It is an hour to arise and shine, for your light has come.

# About Robert Henderson

Robert Henderson is a global apostolic leader who operates in revelation and impartation. His teaching empowers the Body of Christ to see the hidden truths of Scripture clearly and apply them for breakthrough results. Driven by a mandate to disciple nations through writing and speaking, Robert travels extensively around the globe, teaching on the apostolic, the Kingdom of God, the "Seven Mountains," and most notably, the Courts of Heaven. He has been married to Mary for 40 years. They have six children and five grandchildren. Together they are enjoying life in beautiful Midlothian, TX.

# THE YEAR OF TWO POWERS CLASHING

*Prophet Charlie Shamp*

A s I sit down to pen this prophetic word, I recognize the seriousness of the task at hand, for true prophecy must never be speculation but must come from a deep place of revelation. If the Lord does not speak, how can we, if we are His spokesmen, conjecture the future? Prophecy is nether assumption, nor is it presumption; it is the eternal mind of Christ revealing to man the things to come in the future. With that, there will be authentic manifestation.

A person can presume to know what is to come, but this does not make one prophetic; rather, it makes them presumptuous. A true prophet must remain silent until he or she hears His voice, for it is only by waiting through the silence that the truth can be told. As the prophet Isaiah once spoke:

> *The Lord God hath given me the tongue of the learned, that I should know how to speak a word in season to him that is weary: he wakeneth morning by morning, he wakeneth mine ear to hear as the learned. The Lord God hath opened mine ear, and I was not rebellious, neither turned away back* (Isaiah 50:4-5 KJV).

Prophets have one task—to speak on behalf of the King. They can say nothing more and nothing less than those things which they have both seen and heard, because the true test of a prophet is not in the beauty of their delivery, but in the authenticity and accuracy of their words.

I've taken time to highlight several things that I believe will be of key interest in the near future. Some are wonderful things that when I saw them brought great rejoicing to my heart, while others called me to prayer and a place of fasting for nations. The year 2019 will be a year of two great unseen powers clashing—freedom and fear. A great shaking will come upon the nations; some will choose to fear, while others will embrace change and find freedom. Make no mistake—each person will have to choose which they will follow.

On August 12, 2018, I was taken in a very powerful encounter where I saw many United States citizens who were being held captive in foreign nations suddenly set free and sent home. The Lord spoke to me and said:

"**Son, this is the time when many will go free from captivity. It will be seen on every television from sea to shining sea. Those who have been held in chains will break free and receive liberty. Tell the families of those who have been lost and imprisoned for years to get ready for their return. The weeping endured for a night, but joy is breaking through in the dawn of the morn-**

ing. I'm redeeming the land of liberty and releasing the brave to break every chain. For I have raised this President up in righteousness and I will direct all his ways. He will build this nation once again and will let go My captives being held in foreign countries, not for price nor reward. I have not forgotten your sons, your daughters, your husbands; My hand is keeping them in the midst of darkness and I am arising upon them. My redeeming glory will be seen upon them and they will be free! I will do the unprecedented, the unexpected, the unbelievable in the coming days. America, your captives will be free. I will bring them from the nations and gather them from the countries where they have been held captive. With a mighty hand and outstretched arm, I will release them from prison. Do not be afraid, for I am with you; I will bring your children from the East and gather them from the West. I will say to the North, 'Give them up!' and to the South, 'Do not hold them back.' Bring My sons from afar and My daughters from the ends of the earth; they will surely come forth!"

We are coming into a time in human history when we will experience full disclosure on many levels of society. A time of true revealing of things unspoken will come. As the angel spoke to Daniel, *"Shut up the words, and seal the book, even to the time of the end: many shall run to and fro, and knowledge shall be increased"* (Dan. 12:4 KJV). The books of knowledge that have been shut for ages and generations are being opened. We are going to see advancement in technology like we have never seen before, and while we are only focusing on the year 2019, I would be remiss not to say that over the next five years we will see artificial intelligence reach places that just a decade ago would have seemed unrealistic and even fantasy. I saw great advancement in the automotive industry—smart cars that drive themselves will come sooner than any of us could have expected. Aerospace engineering will reach new heights that no one could have projected.

I heard the Lord say:

"I will cause women to do uncommon things in this generation for My glory. They will be clothed with strength and dignity; they will laugh without fear of the future, and freedom will be their portion across the world. They will break new records even in the race to go back to space. For there will be a sign seen from the moon above—yes, humans will once again stand on its surface. I will cause this to mark a great changing of seasons for all of humanity—an expansion of civilization and expansion of human life. This will mark the moment of great change. The sun knows its time for rising and setting, and someday humanity will discover the sun's power in order to harness greater dimensions of energy for the earth."

A great sign will appear in the heavens above; yes, a woman clothed with the energy of the sun, the moon resting under her feet will be seen simultaneously throughout the world. The world will wonder at this sight of the first woman to step foot on the surface of the moon, a Wonder Woman. It will be a marvel and a sign to this generation of an acceleration of technology and life expansion."

In the spirit I could see a new frontier was about to come forth from above. A great new gold rush and the mining of asteroids for materials in space is about to begin. I could see vast amounts of wealth come to the earth as a result of the explorations. I heard the Lord say:

"I will go before them and make all the crooked places straight as they break through to space. Things that could never be understood will suddenly come to light overnight. I will break in pieces the gates of brass over their minds and cut asunder the bars of iron over their heads that have held humans to the earth for so long. I will give them the treasures of darkness and hidden riches of secret places from above that they may know that I the Lord am God."

I could also see down below, in the earth, new technology generating electricity from plant photosynthesis coming forth to produce cleaner energy for the earth. Forests became energy stations of the future. Again I heard the Lord say, "These will be trees of life and the leaves of the tree will be for the healing of the nations." There will be a pressing need for innovation in renewable energy as I saw another oil crisis will arise starting in 2019 as prices and demand begin to rise.

Computer engineering will also soar to unimaginable heights. While your phone and computer don't necessarily seem to be extensions of you, they are and you just haven't realized what is happening. The interface is simply through finger movements or speech, which at this point seem very slow, but what is coming will be as fast as thought. What I was shown in the spirit is an ultra-thin mesh-like material that is implanted in the skull and forms a body of electrodes that are able to monitor brain function. This will cause people to be able flash data from their brains, wirelessly, to their digital devices. I saw a device as small as a contact lens that goes into the eye with full Internet capability. The ultimate goal for some will be to interface technology with humanity completely. These men intend to leave a mark on humanity.

The year 2019, however, will be marked by water. There will be various issues in water and with water that will require much prayer from believers around the world. Flooding will happen in some parts of America as record-breaking rainfall will come. The Church will need to be prepared! On September 3, 2018, the Lord spoke to me and said:

"Place your gaze on the waterways of America; for there will come a crisis once again that will need much prayer to make the water clean and clear. For there will be a contamination in another city's water that will draw great attention. They will say, 'How could it happen here, for our city is so pretty and beauty is all around us, but the ground has become barren and the water is too bad now for us to drink!' Tell My people to stand and pray, and I will reverse the condition that was placed upon that place. My promise still stands if My people, who are called by My name, will humble themselves and pray and seek My face and turn from their wicked ways. Then I will hear from heaven, and I will forgive their sin and will heal their land. Remember, nothing is too far beyond the reach of My hand! I will purify the water of the city for people to drink freely. Just as I touched the waters in Marah with the tree of life. so too will I stretch out My right hand to change the bitter into sweet so people can once again drink. I have called My people to be the salt of the earth and bring healing to the land. As they pray and decree, I will work a wonder in the land; no more death or barrenness will stand. The water will be healed and the land will be redeemed."

My eyes then turned to the west coast of America where I saw vineyards. I heard the Lord say, "Tell My Church that I AM returning to My Vineyard. I am reattaching the branch to the vine." Suddenly I saw a spontaneous move of the Spirit spark in Southern California that touched the Vineyard church. I heard the Lord say, "Signs and wonders will fall and the new wine will flow. It will come to pass that the mountains will drop down new wine, the hills will flow with water, a fountain of life will spring up from this place again, and it will water the whole valley with wonders from above."

I saw the passing of a famous musical artist/pop star that will shock many. I heard the Lord say, "They knew the rhyme, they knew the rhythm, but failed to know it was their time." Many youths will be shocked by the passing of an idol, but their eyes will be opened to how fragile life truly is; some will turn to Christ as a result.

I saw in the spirit that Chechnya and the Northern Caucasus will become a hotbed for radical Islamic terrorism. I was shown a new generation of extremists coming from this part of the world that will make their voices known on the world stage. We must pray for the nation of Russia and their people. As I saw tension arise, an attack in a major city came. Three other nations that will require much prayer against terror attacks will be Egypt, Syria, and Israel. I heard the Lord say, "Blessed be Egypt, My people; watch and pray. Blessed be Syria, the land I will restore. Blessed be Israel, My special possession that My hand is upon." I saw the enemy go to great lengths to bring chaos and terror in these three nations. We must watch and pray!

Also, we can look to 2019 as a year of truth and righteousness. The Lord spoke to me and said, "Many things that have been hidden in the past will be revealed to the public as I bring a frequency of purity into the earth's atmosphere." We will see greater exposure of governmental corruption and manipulation that has been done to America over the past decade. There will be a shaking in the nation as the Lord reveals hidden agendas done to undermine the national security of America—many things will be shaken and exposed as a result of this frequency. Look for a purification to take place on many levels of society. I saw the spirit of perversion exposed in someone who many revere as a powerful person in the world, an untouchable by many standards. They will face the light of what they have done behind closed doors, justice will be done, a sentence will be given, and time will be served.

Lastly, on a personal level look for this frequency of purity to allow a greater place of discernment to be given to you. Such clarity is coming that some will hear the thoughts of others. They will know even when others are lying to them in daily conversations. In this season, God is looking to deposit more than a vision or dream that we can talk about and share with our friends as we drink a Starbucks on a Saturday afternoon. All of that is fine, but we must come to the realization that there is far more that God wants to get over to us. It's not so much what we witness in this coming year that will change us, but what we embrace and receive that will have a lasting impact on us. The deep is calling out to the deep.

It was not until Moses turned aside to see that God called out to him. He was caught up in an ecstatic experience that caused him to awe and wonder, but he did not stop there. He made a decision to dive deeper into what he was encountering, and then God called to him. Many in the Body of Christ are entering past the place of simply encountering and seeing into the heavens to living and working with them.

> *And the angel of the Lord appeared unto him in a flame of fire out of the midst of a bush: and he looked, and, behold, the bush burned with fire, and the bush was not consumed. And Moses said, I will now turn aside, and see this great sight, why the bush is not burnt. And when the Lord saw that he turned aside to see, God called unto him out of the midst of the bush, and said, Moses, Moses. And he said, Here am I* (Exodus 3:2-4 KJV).

Many in the past have known that change was coming to the earth and they even declared what they had seen on the mountain of God, but few have turned to go deeper. God is looking for a people that will not only see, but will embrace and work with Him to bring about a geographical transformation. Both Moses and Isaiah encountered the angel that burns with fire and answered their call with "Here am I." It was not until they fully took hold of what they were seeing and looked deeper into the encounters that God then released a greater deposit on their lives to equip and transform nations. They moved beyond simply seeing to see into receiving to release.

This is where we are heading in the days ahead. The angel of the Lord is being released to work with those who will turn aside. There are men and women who will do mighty exploits for the Kingdom. The nations are going to shake and quake under the supernatural authority that they carry. Look for unusual signs and wonders to come through these mystics and reformers. Many of these wonder-workers we have not heard of before, but they are coming sooner than we think. They will be marked by great humility and simplicity as they manifest the Kingdom of Heaven. They will be given the Rod of God and will deliver many nations from bondage and cause the desire of the nations to come (see Hag. 2:4-9). The Lord is bringing a real shaking that will cause the latter house to arise in all its glory, and at the same time He is releasing a great stirring and shaking that will cause dividing lines within the Body like we have never seen before.

Pay close attention in this coming season to the fault lines. The separation between the old and the new will not come without a price. Fault finding and accusations will be thrown at those who bring about the reformation, transformation, acceleration, but only with persecution comes a greater release of glory (see 1 Pet. 4:12-14). We must not pass up this coming visitation, no matter the cost. For the sake of America and the world we cannot afford to pass up God's opportunity for us and our generation.

# ABOUT CHARLIE SHAMP

CHARLIE SHAMP IS THE CO-FOUNDER AND PRESIDENT OF DESTINY Encounters International. He is a sought-after international keynote speaker. He has been commissioned by Heaven as a Prophet to bring healing and revival in the nations. He has ministered both nationally and internationally with radical demonstrations of faith seeing lives transformed through the power of the Holy Spirit.

# ATTACK, TAKE BACK, AND RECOVER ALL

*Bishop Bill Hamon*

## THE PROPHETIC WORD FOR 2019

The word I gave for the year 2018 is still active for those who are still co-laboring with Christ to fulfill His present purpose for His Church. The word of the Lord was and still is "the most glorious and prosperous time."

I started giving a prophetic word for the year in 1988. I first gave the word just for Christian International, but in the 1990s I expanded it to our nation and nations of the world. Then some of my prophetic ministers started giving a word for the year, and now in the 21st century prophetic ministers around the world are doing the same. Many of the words given are quite revealing and are coming to pass. In the year 2000, we started printing all the words CI ministers gave in a magazine or booklet form.

We discovered that the word was given for that year, but it could take several years for it to be completely fulfilled. The word for the year usually speaks of specific things, but also reveals a new season beginning for the progressive purpose of God to be fulfilled on the earth.

This year, I felt the Lord wanted me to cover the word of the Lord for the Church to know the new beginnings in 2019. My daughter, Jane Hamon, has received revelation on the number nine using the ninth hour of prayer, which reveals many things God wants to do in 2019. I have some words concerning the President and some nations, etc., but I am leaving that to some of my prophet friends like Lance Wallnau who has the word of the Lord for the President.

The following are a few things that are being started, activated, and intensified this year.

The glory of the Lord is the personification of the life of Christ, the manifestation of Christ's ministry, and the working of His mighty wonders. What has now begun will continue to grow and spread until the glory of the Lordship of Jesus Christ fills the earth as the waters cover the sea (see Hab. 2:14, Num. 14:21).

The light, glory, and power of the Kingdom of God is arising like a great tsunami. The Kingdom of God will be demonstrated with miracles and such accurate prophecies that demonstrate the Lordship of Jesus Christ until every nation has a witness that Jehovah Jesus is the true and only God of heaven and earth (see Matt. 24:14; Dan. 4:34-37; 6:24-28).

We must know God's times and purposes. Israel did not recognize God's time for their Messiah to be manifest on the earth. They missed their day of visitation, which caused Jesus to pronounce judgment upon them. This resulted in their temple being destroyed and the nation of Israel being dissolved—not to be restored until almost two thousand years later in 1948 (see Luke 19:44).

God planned three separate periods of time to accomplish His purpose in and through His mortal Church. The first period of time is called the First Reformation. Its purpose was to send Jesus to birth the Church, establish it, and then take it to every person under the sun. That took about 500 years to accomplish (see Acts 20:28; Col. 1:23; Eph. 4:11-15; Matt. 16:18).

The Second Reformation was purposed to restore back to the Church all ministries and truths that were preached and practiced in the New Testament. This was accomplished in 500 years from 1517 to 2017 (see Joel 2:25; Acts 3:21).

The Third and Final Church Reformation was birthed in 2008 and by 2017 was being taught around the world. God's purpose for the Third and Final Reformation is to activate and demonstrate all that has been restored into the Church, enabling the Church to demonstrate the Kingdom and fulfill all end-time purposes God has ordained for the Church to fulfill up until Jesus' second coming (see Acts 3:21; Heb. 10:12-13; Rev. 11:15).

Know that we are not in the First Reformation of the Church or the thousand-year Dark Age or the Second Reformation of the Church Restoration, but in the Third Reformation where the fulfillment and finalizing of all things will take place. We need to know the times and be established in the present truth (see 2 Pet. 1:12; 1 Thess. 5:1-6; Eph. 1:10).

Knowing and fulfilling God's present purpose can determine our future.

Jesus is arising as the Mighty Man of War to raise up His army—an army of prophets who will demonstrate His Kingdom in and prophesy His word to every nation. How the nations respond, either turning to Jesus or rebelling against God's word, will determine whether they will end up being a goat nation or a sheep nation. One of the first things that Jesus is going to do when He returns is bring all nations before Him and let them know whether they are a sheep nation or a goat nation and why they are receiving a blessing or a judgment (see Matt. 25:31; Rev. 21:24). Prophets to the nations are now prophesying. The prophecies of the Old Testament prophets determined the destiny of that nation. (Numerous examples are found in the books of the major prophets.)

In 2019, like David after Ziklag, we are receiving the same word of the Lord that David then received. In other words, this is the action we, the Church, are to take against our enemies who have stolen from us—*attack, take back, and recover all!* (See 1 Samuel 30:8; 17-20.)

In 2019, saints who are overcomers are coming to level three. We have been overcoming by the 1) blood of the Lamb, 2) word of our testimony, 3) and now we must love not our lives unto death. That means complete death to self, life in the spirit, and conformity to the character of Christ (see Rev. 12:11; Gal. 2:20; 2 Cor. 4:10-11).

We have entered the second wave of the prophetic. The first phase was the birthing of the prophetic movement in 1988. Then there was a noising abroad and a coming together and forming a Body of prophets and prophetic people who formed networks. But now, over 30 years later, we are commanded to prophesy again until resurrection life is activated into the Body of Christ and the Church arises as an exceeding great army (see Ezek. 37:10).

In 2019, the final and most important thing to know is this: God's highest calling and purpose for every saint and minister is for them to be conformed to the likeness of Jesus Christ. God needs a certain number of His people, who obtain maturity in Christ Jesus and are overcomers, to become joint heirs and co-laborers with Christ for the purpose of ruling and reigning with Christ and maintaining His Kingdom throughout the endless ages (see Eph. 3:11; Rom. 8:17; Rev. 2 and 3; Rev. 21:7).

In 2019, the Holy Spirit is beginning an intensified work to purify and perfect us to Christ's likeness and maturity. If you are one of those chosen for this purpose, then believe Romans 8:28 is working to fulfill Romans

8:29. We must develop Paul's conviction in Romans 8:18 that the suffering of the flesh crucifying process that it takes to transform us into Christ's maturity is not worthy to be compared with the glory that shall be revealed in and through us. For Romans 8:19 declares that the whole creation is anxiously waiting for God's elect to reach that maturity and manifestation of the fullness of Christ's glory. Allow the following scriptures to become a living reality in your life—Galatians 2:20; 2 Corinthians 4:10-11; Colossians 3:3-4,10; Romans 12:1 2; Ephesians 4:13-15.

The Church has entered the Third and Final Reformation that began in 2008. Too many ministers are just maintainers of old restored truths. God is looking for pioneers and Third Reformation Reformers to help Him fulfill His purpose for the Third Reformation, which is revealing all the mysteries, fulfilling all end-time prophetic scriptures, and finalizing all things necessary for the second coming of Christ Jesus (see Acts 3:21; Heb. 10:12 13; Rev. 10:7; Eph. 3:5-6, 9-11).

# ABOUT BISHOP BILL HAMON

DR. BILL HAMON IS THE FOUNDER OF CHRISTIAN INTERNATIONAL Ministries. A prophet for over 60 years, he has prophesied to more than 50,000 people and provided training for over 250,000 in prophetic ministry. He has authored seven major books, specializing in the restoration of the Church and what to expect next on God's agenda.

Dr. Bill Hamon is respected by church leaders around the world as the senior leader of the prophetic/apostolic company God is raising up in these last days. Dr. Hamon was recently featured by *Charisma* Magazine as one of the 40 people who radically changed the Church.

He serves as bishop to over 800 minsters and churches in the United States as well as over 3,000 ministries overseas via Christian International's headquarters around the world. Dr. Hamon resides in Santa Rosa Beach, Florida. He has three children, eleven grandchildren and sixteen great-grandchildren.

# 2019: The Year of the Decree

*Jennifer LeClaire*

I DECREE AND DECLARE." THESE ARE FOUR WORDS WE HEAR prayer warriors cry out in the heat of the battle—but often without an experiential revelation of the power of a decree.

In 2019, God will demonstrate the power of a decree with rapid breakthrough following. He is pouring out revelation on Job 22:28 to believers who can believe Christ's delegated authority positions us as more than priests who petition—but kings who decree and see an immediate response in the natural realm. I heard the Lord say:

"Far too many of My people are begging Me to do what I've already promised I would do. Far too many are making supplication, bargaining with Me to do My revealed will, petitioning and crying out from a place of hope instead of faith. But I am calling My body to rise up and decree what I have already said, to prophesy what I've already said, to declare what I've already said, and to see My will and My Kingdom established in the earth. There is a time for every purpose under heaven. There's a time to pray the prayer of faith. There's a time to war with a prophetic word. There's a time to make supplication. There's a time to release the prayer of consecration. But in this season I am demonstrating the power of a decree released by the leading of My Spirit through a heart of faith. Decree a thing and it shall be established."

Job 22:28 assures us, *"Thou shalt also decree a thing, and it shall be established unto thee: and the light shall shine upon thy ways"* (KJV). Different translations shed interesting light on this verse. For example, the New International Version tells us, *"What you decide on will be done, and light will shine on your ways."* The Contemporary English Version puts it this way: *"He will do whatever you ask, and life will be bright."*

The Amplified Bible, Classic Edition expounds on this truth a little more: *"You shall also decide and decree a thing, and it shall be established for you; and the light [of God's favor] shall shine upon your ways."* And *The Message* assures, *"You'll decide what you want and it will happen; your life will be bathed in light."*

## What Is a Decree?

We can decree the Word of God or the revealed will of God through prophecy. There is power in the Word of God. Heaven and earth will pass away, but His Word will never pass away (see Matt. 24:35). His Word is life to all those who find it and healing to the flesh (see Prov. 4:22). His Word will add length to your life and give you peace (see Prov. 3:2). The grass withers and the flowers fade away, but the Word of God will stand forever (see Isa. 40:8). His Word is spirit and life (see John 6:63). His Word is truth (see John 17:17). His Word is pure, like silver tried in a furnace, purified seven times (see Ps. 12:6).

Hebrews 4:11-16 explains:

> *Let us labor therefore to enter that rest, lest anyone fall by the same pattern of unbelief. For the word of God is alive, and active, and sharper than any two-edged sword, piercing even to the division of soul and spirit, of joints and marrow, and able to judge the thoughts and intents of the heart. There is no creature that is not revealed in His sight, for all things are bare and exposed to the eyes of Him to whom we must give account.*
>
> *Since then we have a great High Priest who has passed into the heavens, Jesus the Son of God, let us hold firmly to our confession. For we do not have a High Priest who cannot sympathize with our weaknesses, but One who was in every sense tempted like we are, yet without sin. Let us then come with confidence to the throne of grace, that we may obtain mercy and find grace to help in time of need* (MEV).

A decree is more than a positive confession. A decree is an order usually having the force of law, according to Webster's dictionary. God expects us to follow His decrees (see Lev. 18:4). The enemy is also bound to obey a prophetic declaration in the name of Jesus, the name at which every knee must bow and every tongue confess that He is Lord (see Rom. 14:11).

## You Are a Priest and a King

Believers have a duality of standing in the role of both kings and priests. Jesus is the King of kings and the Lord of lords (see Rev. 17:14). Who are these kings who report to the King? We are. Revelation 1:6 says He has made us *"kings and priests to His God and Father"* (MEV). Let me share with you a few scriptures that bring this point home.

> *For if by one man's trespass death reigned through him, then how much more will those who receive abundance of grace and the gift of righteousness reign in life through the One, Jesus Christ* (Romans 5:17 MEV).

> *But you are a chosen race, a royal priesthood, a holy nation, a people for God's own possession, so that you may declare the goodness of Him who has called you out of darkness into His marvelous light* (1 Peter 2:9 MEV).

Priests don't have power in government. Kings do. Governmental intercessors don't pray with a priestly anointing alone; they pray with a kingly anointing. Still, most intercessors stand in the role of priest. We need to understand when to make the shift between the priestly mantle and the kingly mantle—when to operate in the anointing of the priest and the anointing of a king.

Kings have a domain in which they exercise authority (see 2 Cor. 10:3). Kings have power and influence. Kings are warriors who defend a nation against its enemies. Kings govern and uphold laws. Kings oversee administrations. Kings establish order and maintain peace, when possible. Kings judge and decree. Throughout the Bible we see kings issuing decrees:

> *We are the servants of the God of heaven and earth and are rebuilding the temple that was built these many years ago, which a great king of Israel built and completed. Afterwards,*

*our fathers provoked the God of heaven to wrath, so He gave them into the hand of Nebuchadnezzar the king of Babylon, the Chaldean, who destroyed this temple and carried the people away into Babylon. However, in the first year of Cyrus the king of Babylon, King Cyrus made a decree to rebuild this house of God* (Ezra 5:11-13 MEV).

We see what happened next in Ezra 6: "*Then Darius the king issued a decree and a search was made in the house of records, where the treasures were stored in Babylon*" (Ezra 6:1 MEV). King Cyrus' decree was found and Darius enforced it.

## DECREES CANNOT BE UNDONE

In the book of Esther, King Ahasuerus made a decree that his wife, Vashti, could never enter into his presence again (see Esther 1:19). She never did. Haman later persuaded Ahasuerus to issue an evil decree to wipe out the Jews (see Esther 3:8). Ahasuerus could not undo his original decree, but Esther convinced him to issue a second decree that gave the Jews a right to defend themselves against enemy attack (see Esther 8:11).

In Daniel 3, we learn that King Nebuchadnezzar issued a decree "*that every man who hears the sound of the cornet, flute, harp, sackbut, psaltery, and dulcimer, and all kinds of music should fall down and worship the golden image. And whoever does not fall down and worship should be cast into the midst of a burning fiery furnace*" (Daniel 3:10-11 MEV). That decree could not be undone, and it landed Shadrach, Meshach, and Abednego in a fiery furnace, but God delivered them from the evil decree.

Later, King Darius' officials unknowingly convinced him to make a decree against Daniel:

*"All the presidents of the kingdom, the governors, and the officials, the counselors, and the captains have consulted together*

*to establish a royal statute and to make a firm decree, that whoever shall ask a petition of any god or man for thirty days, save of you, O king, shall be cast into the den of lions. Now, O king, establish the decree and sign the writing, that it not be changed, according to the law of the Medes and Persians, which may not be altered." Therefore King Darius signed the writing, even the decree* (Daniel 6:7-9 MEV).

Daniel refused to compromise. Darius didn't want to throw him in the lion's den but he could not negate the decree. When he saw the power of God in Daniel's situation, Darius made another decree:

*Then King Darius wrote: To all peoples, nations, and languages that dwell in all the earth. "Peace be multiplied unto you. I make a decree that in every dominion of my kingdom men are to fear and tremble before the God of Daniel. For He is the living God, enduring forever; His kingdom shall never be destroyed, and His dominion shall be forever. He delivers and rescues, and He works signs and wonders in heaven and on earth, who has delivered Daniel from the power of the lions"* (Daniel 6:25-27).

Again, Job 22:28 assures us, *"Thou shalt also decree a thing, and it shall be established unto thee: and the light shall shine upon thy ways"* (KJV). *Gazar* is the Hebrew word for decree. It means, "to cut, divide, cut down, cut off, cut in two, snatch." When we decree, we are cutting off the enemy's plan and establishing God's will. God Himself declares:

*For as the rain comes down, and the snow from heaven, and do not return there but water the earth and make it bring forth and bud that it may give seed to the sower and bread to the eater, so shall My word be that goes forth from My mouth; it shall not return to Me void, but it shall accomplish that which I please, and it shall prosper in the thing for which I sent it* (Isaiah 55:10-11 MEV).

My prayer is that you will learn to discern in any situation when it's time to pray as a priest and when it's time to pray as a king. In this year, God is demonstrating the power of a decree because a decree can be the tipping point to a bowl filled with intercession.

# About Jennifer LeClaire

Jennifer is senior leader of Awakening House of Prayer in Fort Lauderdale, FL, founder of the Ignite Network and founder of the Awakening Blaze prayer movement. Jennifer formerly served as the first-ever female editor of *Charisma* magazine and is a prolific author of over 25 books. You can find Jennifer online or shoot her an email at info@jenniferleclaire.org.

# A SEASON OF GRACE TO PREPARE

*R. Loren Sandford*

UNDER THE PRESIDENCY OF DONALD TRUMP, WE LIVE IN A SEAson of grace and favor that we must use to prepare for the coming full manifestation of Isaiah 60:1-3:

> *Arise, shine; for your light has come, and the glory of the Lord has risen upon you. For behold, darkness will cover the earth and deep darkness the peoples; but the Lord will rise upon you and His glory will appear upon you. Nations will come to your light, and kings to the brightness of your rising.*

I expect this window in time to begin to expire in 2020 coinciding with the heat of the next presidential election, unless extended by the fervent prayers of the remnant faithful. In any case, the fourth year of the President's term will involve turmoil and we will need to be ready to walk a godly path in the midst of it.

This makes the days that lie immediately before us vitally and strategically important, perhaps at a higher level and to a greater degree than at any time since World War II. The period of time represented by 2019 (God's calendar doesn't conform to ours) will seem to be a kind of rising plateau of economic prosperity as well as improved conditions in the world. It will be a time of relative stability, perhaps punctuated by the usual sorts of brief eruptions of trouble and a continuation of "Trump Derangement Syndrome" on the part of the left—while in reality this is a turning point season that will determine whether this window of grace will be extended or come to an early end.

Ultimately and inevitably, darkness and deep darkness will cover the nations, but the coming darkness will also be the time of our greatest shining and resounding victory, provided we prepare effectively.

I see these days as a sort of nexus in time, a narrow passage with a decisive and significant outcome. As we pass through this era—however long it lasts—what is done, negotiated, legislated, and accepted or rejected will have historically profound effects on the direction of our nation and the world, as well as on the manner in which the world regards Christians. How we carry ourselves as believers in our devotion, faithfulness, holiness, and purity of love for one another and for those outside will determine whether we become a minor and despised religious cult or the world's greatest change agent. The decisions we make as believers, as well as the depths of relationship we cultivate with Jesus and one another, will have far-reaching consequences.

Regardless of what you might think of Donald Trump overall, in contrast to the previous administration we have a President who favors both the Church and Israel. *"Pray for the peace of Jerusalem: 'May they prosper who love you. May peace be within your walls, and prosperity within your palaces'"* (Ps. 122:6-7). God deals with His people according the condition of their relationship with Him. He deals with nations according to how they treat His people. The previous administration did not treat God's people favorably. By contrast, Trump blesses and supports both the Church and Israel. This reaps blessing for our nation.

We who follow Jesus have therefore been granted a window of grace in which to prosper economically and to have a growing impact on the world around us at every level. In order to make that impact, we must take holiness and integrity seriously or be discredited in the eyes of the world. At the present moment the church in general is not seen as a source of grace, love, and reconciliation, but rather as judgmental, harsh, and unloving toward those we deem less holy. This must be remedied. This is a time to diligently pursue a purity of focus on Jesus and His character written into us through His Spirit who sanctifies. *"For those whom He foreknew, He also predestined to become conformed to the image of His Son"* (Rom. 8:29). A people who look like Jesus will impact the world like Jesus.

## A Fresh Strategy

On that note, this is the strategic hour for the Josephs and the Daniels of our day to emerge and exert influence on governors and kings. This can only be done, not by crying out in bitter and judgmental tones against the unrighteous and those with whom we disagree, but by adopting the strategies of Joseph, Daniel, and even the early Christians under Roman domination. Both Joseph and Daniel suffered injustice under godless and immoral rulers, but rather than feast on negativity they chose to serve. They used their spiritual gifts to benefit those who ruled over them, and in the process they caused the ungodly to acknowledge the God of heaven while saving the lives of the Lord's own people.

The early Christians took a similar approach, applied somewhat differently. While Rome persecuted believers in Jesus and wallowed in immorality and corruption, Christians chose to love rather than react in bitterness. When plagues came to Rome, Roman families abandoned even their own, casting them out into the streets in the attempt to avoid becoming sick themselves. By contrast, the Christians went out in groups to seek out the sick in order to take them in and care for them. By the end of the third century they became the dominant faith in the empire through love.

In order to effectively adopt the strategy of the early Christians, we must first recognize that we live in a post-Christian culture. At a cultural level, America, for instance, is no longer the Christian nation it once was. If we cry out for sinners to miraculously start acting like Christians, proclaiming judgment on a godless culture, thinking that by doing so we will inspire the nation to repentance and a return to its Christian roots, we will only sound hateful and harsh. We will be guilty of misrepresenting our Lord and will turn the hearts of both society and government against us. We must rather draw so close to Jesus with such a pure focus on intimacy with Him that we radiate the kind of glory, beauty, and love that actually wins hearts and influences nations.

The wave of hatred currently engulfing America and the world will continue to grow. Whether or not we Christians succumb to it and become participants in it will determine whether we become world changers or merely a forgotten and despised minority. I believe God is calling a remnant of dedicated disciples to become the former, but we need a change of strategy. Sinners come to repentance because they feel the Father's love flowing from Jesus through us, not by being confronted, judged, and condemned.

Holy Spirit brings conviction by means of exposure to the light that reveals darkness to be darkness.

> *But I tell you the truth, it is to your advantage that I go away; for if I do not go away, the Helper will not come to you; but if I go, I will send Him to you. And He, when He comes, will convict the world concerning sin and righteousness and judgment* (John 16:7-8).

We can never win by usurping the function the Holy Spirit has reserved to Himself. It's not our job to bring conviction. It's our job to love. The Holy Spirit brings conviction. Inspiration to turn away from sin comes not by crying out against sin but by revealing the goodness of our Lord. His goodness exposes shades of darkness that people have been conditioned to think of as light. Watch for a movement of repentance to take root, even among believers, that comes as the result of waves of powerful revelation of the Father's goodness and love.

## THREE PROPHETIC MANDATES FOR PREPARATION

In 2015 I had a series of three prophetic dreams representing three mandates for the Church that have become much more vital for these days of preparation than they were when I had them.

### *Mandate #1*

I dreamed that I was speaking for a meeting of a small group of people when the senior pastor of a mega-church I once served as the executive pastor walked in. I had been badly wounded and even slandered during my brief sojourn there, and he and I had not parted on good terms. Despite my overtures for reconciliation, we have not spoken or seen one another in 27 years.

As he entered the room, however, he was once more my friend, greeting me cordially. He joked that we had been a bit crazy during the Toronto

Blessing in the church I planted after I left him. During that season, he had publicly slandered us, but as we talked I good-naturedly agreed that we were, indeed, a bit out of the box. We both laughed. The musicians in that former church were top pros in the Christian music and worship arena. Just being around them challenged me to catch up. They inspired me to become a better musician, and as a result I now have 14 CDs in release. I thanked him for that.

Then he took me to see a nephew of his at his nephew's apartment. There I saw a room filled with TV screens and big windows running down two sides of a messy room.

The mandate symbolized in this dream is this. If we would prepare effectively for the days to come, we must forgive old church wounds and reconcile with those who have perpetrated them. The Body of Christ must heal and come together as one in honor of the prayer of Jesus, *"that they may all be one"* (John 17:21). This speaks not only to the unity of the Body of Christ, but also clearly affects the credibility of our witness to the world concerning Jesus. See the last half of that verse!

Further, the generation to come is a prophetic one, as symbolized by the TV screens and windows. We must reconcile with one another and heal the Church for the sake of the young, understanding that they are indeed messy, but loving them just the same. As a last days generation they carry a prophetic gifting, as messy as they may seem to us older ones. We must transcend our old hurts, get over ourselves, and come together as the Body of Christ to provide the platform and the safety the young need in order to grow into their callings.

## Mandate #2

I dreamed that I was walking through a large indoor shopping mall where President Obama was about to give an address to the nation expressing his sorrow over the mass shootings we have seen in recent years. I approached the place of the filming and found there was just one secret service man there to guard the President. As I got closer, the Lord filled me with an overwhelming love for Barak Obama, a man with whom I had strenuous disagreements over his policies. To my discredit, my attitude toward him had often bordered on hatred, but I found myself overflowing with love and compassion.

I walked right past the secret service man, approached the President, and said, "Would it be all right if I stood with you before the people?" Tears filled his eyes and he grasped my hands like a drowning man and said, "Yes!" I told the stage hands to remove the lectern so that we could be seen unimpeded standing together before the nation to make the announcement.

The mandate embedded in this dream is that we as believers have come into a time when we must see those whom we have bitterly opposed as the human beings they are. Jesus died for their sins, too. We must learn to love them with the Father's love if we are to have the impact we're called and destined to have in the coming days. Kings will not come to the brightness of our rising if all they sense in us is hatred and condemnation. This does not mean that we compromise our commitments. Daniel certainly didn't compromise his, and yet he chose to serve Nebuchadnezzar, the king who destroyed his homeland and sought to erase his Jewish identity. As a result, that king came to the brightness of Daniel's rising.

## Mandate #3

After John Paul Jackson's passing, it was as though he came to me in a dream for counsel. I was deeply impacted emotionally as he poured out his grief and brokenness over what he saw going on in the prophetic movement that he could no longer do anything about. I knew in the dream that he had passed away, so it felt as though his spirit had come to me with the grief one might feel when going back to fix old errors was no longer possible. I felt the weight of a responsibility being passed to me that affected me for days afterward.

God has issued a mandate to the Body of Christ to clean up prophetic ministry. A shift in the prophetic world is already under way and will accelerate in the coming days, moving us toward prophetic voices we can trust. A generation of those whose words have not proven to be consistently accurate is being retired. Those who have promoted abusive practices and promoted unbiblical approaches, skewed doctrines, and self-aggrandizement are passing away or experiencing diminished influence.

Please know that I'm not lumping together all those who are aging or passing away. I can think of a number who blazed trails for the rest of us— men and women of character, humility, and purity of devotion to Jesus. A new generation, however, more grounded in the heart of the Father and in His written Word, now rises. At this writing they're mostly hidden, not mainstream, and not well-known, but they will emerge to increased prominence in the coming months and years.

Those we might see as mainstream voices may sell books and pack conferences, but accuracy and substance have often been lacking. A different heart has taken root in this upcoming generation. As the Micaiahs of our day, they stand alone among the 400, getting it right but not truly received by the kings in authority. Those older prophetic voices who carry over into this shift will be seasoned mentors with the heart of the Father to father a generation of more accurate prophetic voices emerging at just the right time in history.

The mandate for the Body of Christ is to hold prophetic people accountable. We need checks and balances on our character, truth spoken in love. When we get it wrong, we need to be told so that we can examine ourselves and learn why we were in error. I realize that in Bible times prophets trained prophets, just as Elijah trained Elisha, but in the New Testament paradigm God's people play an equally important role.

## AVOID SPIRITUAL SLUMBER

A sense of security created by growing economic prosperity in these coming days can dull our sense of the urgency of the hour. If we allow a spirit of slumber to overtake us we court defeat and disaster in the coming days of darkness over the world. We can shine in the darkness, influence nations, and draw multitudes of hurting sinners to Jesus only if we have adequately prepared ourselves to do so. Unfortunately, too much of the Church remains sound asleep and unresponsive at a time when we desperately need to be alert in spirit, using this window of favor to focus on prayer, repentance, and purified devotion to Jesus.

Prophetic voices must play a key role in crying out for awakening, holiness, and repentance. Even now these voices emerge, although it might seem not in great numbers. After all, the true prophets of the Old Testament were ever and always in the minority. In First Kings 22 Ahab would have lived had he listened to the solitary voice of Micaiah standing alone against the 400. God calls for a generation of genuine prophets in the tradition of Elijah, Isaiah, Jeremiah, and Ezekiel, unafraid to separate the precious from the vile, even it makes them unpopular.

In addition to spiritual preparation, it would be a good idea to use this time of economic favor to get out of debt before the current economic blessing dissipates.

## CIVIL WAR IN THE BODY OF CHRIST

A remnant of precious saints understand the need to prepare and have therefore chosen to actively engage in seeking the Lord in purity and depth. Look, however, for the quiet civil war under way in the Body of Christ to intensify as the canyon of separation between two camps, two brands of Christianity, grows wider and deeper. On the one side will be the proponents of hyper-grace who distort the Father's love while ignoring passages of Scripture that portray Him as Judge or as a Father who disciplines His children. On this same side of the canyon are increasing numbers of those who succumb to societal pressures to compromise clear biblical mandates concerning morality. Increasing numbers of pastors and leaders will come out in support of gay marriage, for instance, and will justify their apostasy on the grounds of God's love and grace.

Aberrant and unbiblical theologies have already taken root in Christian circles and will proliferate, hyper-grace among them, but there are others as well. Universalism—the idea that everyone goes to heaven because of what Jesus did, repentant or not, receiving Him or not—is gaining ground among many we once considered solid leaders. Open theism was sown into the church some years ago. Open theists teach that God does not know the end from the beginning, which by any standard of reasoning negates His omniscience. Many more who claim to be followers of Jesus will teach that there are multiple paths to God in denial of the truth that no one comes to the Father but by Jesus.

On the other side of the divide are those who stand for the true revelation of our Triune God that changes lives and calls us to higher places of holiness and love. These hold to the plumb line of the faith once delivered and the truth of infallible Scripture. They stand for biblical morality, refusing to reinterpret or overlook what God has clearly stated, knowing that obedience to Jesus is the only true freedom and that God gave every moral law to bless, protect, and prosper us. Those who stand do so without succumbing to hate or the errors of the Pharisees. Love marks their path, but without compromise of what they know to be true. Yes, we can love homosexuals and child-molesters and drug addicts and thieves and liars and domestic abusers and more without compromising our principles. Disagreement with a lifestyle does not negate love.

The contrast and distance between these two groups will widen while yet another chasm develops. On one side will be those who claim to be "seeker sensitive," limiting worship services to an hour—15 minutes of songs and a fluffy sermon with very little challenge to discipleship or time devoted to ushering people into the raw presence of God where He is free to move. On the other side will be a hungry and passionate remnant who prize extended worship pursued until breakthrough into the presence. One group will continue to attend one-hour worship services with three songs and a nice sermon while the remnant prays all night and worships until their voices grow hoarse. Rejecting hype, performance, rote, and routine, this group hungers for the genuine and will accept nothing less. Passionately in love with Jesus, with His people, and with prayer, this group will see an increased outpouring of the Spirit of God, together with manifestations of the Kingdom in signs and wonders—a mere rehearsal for the glory days to come.

## EMERGING LEADERSHIP

God is now, and will be, moving the pieces on His master chessboard to position us for strategic days of change, glory, and impact. Ministries are shifting in spirit, practice, and leadership. Those who embrace His changes to reflect His heart more fully will prosper, even though the process of change may be gut-wrenching and difficult. Some will see losses before they see gains as the Lord moves His people through the process of change. Those who miss it or reject the manifestation of His heart and the changes it brings will be retired or significantly diminished. Ministries very close to me and my heart have already diminished in influence or have closed altogether.

Fresh ministries will emerge, and are now emerging, to carry the new anointing forward in new wineskins able to stretch and contain what God will be doing. It is a season, not just for the revelation of who He really is but for His people to walk in it. I see this as both a prophetic promise and a warning. Something big is in the works, and I want to be part of it.

Prophetic voices and leaders who carry the Father's heart will increasingly emerge while others fade away as the Lord shifts leadership in the Body of Christ. A new generation with a purified heart for God and His people, as well as a commitment to the infallible Scriptures, is even now emerging. Names you've never heard will ascend to the national and international spotlight. They've labored in small places, out of the public eye as the Lord has prepared them in the wilderness, refining their character for the calling that lies ahead. Most will be age 40 and under. Those of us who remain of the older generation are called as spiritual fathers to nurture and undergird these younger ones who will likely become bigger names, more recognized on the world stage than we who taught them will ever be. We will need to take our joy from seeing them advance. Humility is essential.

# ABOUT R. LOREN SANDFORD

R. LOREN SANDFORD HAS BEEN IN FULL-TIME MINISTRY SINCE 1976 and is a long time international leader in renewal, as well as a prophetic voice. He is the founding pastor of New Song Church and Ministries in Denver, Colorado where he continues to serve, travels and teaches internationally and has authored a number of books.

# An Hour for Revelatory Wisdom and Knowledge

*Adam F. Thompson*

> Many will be purified, made spotless and refined, but the
> wicked will continue to be wicked. None of the wicked
> will understand, but those who are wise will understand.
> —Daniel 12:10 NIV

THIS IS THE HOUR FOR THE CHURCH OF JESUS CHRIST TO FIRMLY position itself in the revelatory knowledge and wisdom of God. I believe we are now living in the time and the circumstances that Daniel the prophet was referring to. *"None of the wicked will understand, but those who are wise will understand"* (Dan. 12:10 NIV).

Earlier in the same chapter God instructed Daniel that this information was to be sealed until the end times. *"But you, Daniel, roll up and seal the words of the scroll until the time of the end. Many will go here and there to increase knowledge"* (Dan. 12:4 NIV).

In the space of the last 115 years the increase of knowledge has intensified dramatically, particularly in the expression of advanced technology. We have seen the Wright brothers' invention of the flying machine and the breaking of the laws of gravity. We witnessed man walking on the moon. We have the daily experience of holding in the palm of our hands Steve Jobs' little flat-screen TV, which enables instant communication with each other even from the other side of the planet. Only 30 years ago much of the technology we take for granted today would have seemed surreal, the stuff of fantasy fiction.

There is nothing new under the sun. From the Garden of Eden and the Tree of Knowledge until the present time, human beings have tried to subvert God's wisdom and walk in their own puny understanding. There has always been a contest between human wisdom and the wisdom that comes only from God. In Exodus, we read of Moses and Aaron petitioning the Pharaoh of the time for the release of their people.

> *So Moses and Aaron went to Pharaoh and did just as the Lord commanded. Aaron threw his staff down in front of Pharaoh and his officials, and it became a snake. Pharaoh then summoned wise men and sorcerers, and the Egyptian magicians also did the same things by their secret arts: Each one threw down his staff and it became a snake. But Aaron's staff swallowed up their staffs* (Exodus 7:10-12 NIV).

When Aaron's rod was thrown down at Pharaoh's feet and became a snake, Pharaoh quickly summoned his magicians. He wanted to engage in a contest that would place a question mark over God's authority. This is what is happening in the present age. The same anti-Christ spirit that was in Pharaoh now uses technology to desensitize people to the power of God. This is why the Church must come into its place of godly wisdom. As the sons of darkness are coming to maturity, so must the sons of light. The earth is groaning for the sons of God to rise up to full stature.

We are at a place in time like Mount Carmel, where people will no longer waver between two opinions. I believe the Church will learn to move not only in supernatural power but also to mature in the wisdom and love of God. God is both love and wisdom, but it is not the wisdom of the world. The enemy can counterfeit signs and wonders, but he can't counterfeit the love of God or His wisdom.

The maturity that the Body of Christ is coming into is the culmination of its governmental role in the earth. The Body will be raised up in such authority that the world will begin to look to it for answers. The influence of prophets like Daniel and Joseph is well-documented in the biblical records of their own times, but I believe their lives were parables or prophetic signs that point to our own era. I see that prophets like them are being raised up to demonstrate how the Body of Christ is to influence the world.

Daniel and his friends were captives in Nebuchadnezzar's palace, compelled to comply with Babylonian ways, but even in the midst of that they walked in knowledge and true understanding from God. Daniel also had the wisdom to understand dreams and visions. When Nebuchadnezzar summoned these young Israelites for questioning he was impressed. He recognized they were ten times wiser than any of the Babylonian wise men who advised him. Then, in Daniel 2, we are told the king had a puzzling dream. Frustrated by his advisors' habit of telling him only what they thought he wanted to hear, he insisted they must first tell him the actual content of this dream. Furthermore, he pronounced that if they could not do so, they would be executed.

Daniel and his friends immediately sought the Lord for revelatory knowledge. When Daniel came before the king he was able to describe the dream of the statue and its separate parts, which represented the superpowers to come—the head of gold, which represented Babylon at that time; the silver torso (Persia); the bronze thighs (Greece); and the iron legs (Rome); all of which, as we know, came to pass.

Historically, the final section of the statue—the toes of iron mixed with clay—has been interpreted in several ways. It is my belief it represents the present era of extreme technology, with clay as a metaphor for man—we know from Scripture that the Lord created man (Adam) from clay—and iron representing technology, specifically robotic machinery. We might picture this as a creature of iron covered with skin, as seen in the worldly movie *The Terminator*. It is my conviction that the iron mixed with clay is a metaphor for artificial intelligence (AI). By heavenly revelation, Daniel was able to prophesy that this union between humans and machines would ultimately end in failure.

> *And as you saw the iron mixed with common clay, so they will combine with one another in the seed of men; but they will not merge [for such diverse things or ideologies cannot unite], even as iron does not mix with clay* (Daniel 2:43 AMP)

It is my belief that in 2019 we will see an even more rapid development of technology—particularly in AI—so rapid it will seem like a sudden flick of a switch. It will quickly escalate into a contest with the Holy Spirit's power in signs, wonders, and miracles. However, as Daniel goes on to tell the king—and us—this union of man and technology will quickly come to an end when it is utterly shattered by the Rock. The Rock, of course, is Jesus Christ, the Messiah. I am so blessed every time I read this revelation!

Through the Body of His people, the Church, Jesus will destroy the enemy's plans for a counterfeit kingdom and reestablish His eternal Kingdom. He will do this not only by the superiority of His power and love but also by downloading to His people the wisdom to govern. He will give supernatural answers to the problems being experienced by the nations of the earth.

In Joseph we see another picture of the wisdom to govern that is given to God's yielded ones in dangerous times. Joseph was betrayed by his brothers, thrown into a pit, and eventually promoted to sit on the right hand of Pharaoh's throne. With this authority to govern, his wisdom was sought after by the whole known world. Joseph's life wasn't just a prophetic outline of the coming Messiah; I believe it is a blueprint for how the Body of Christ will function in the earth.

In the New Testament, Stephen—who himself was recorded as a man whose wisdom could not be resisted—reminds us that Joseph had wisdom that only came from above (see Acts 7:9). The deal clincher was not simply that Joseph could interpret Pharaoh's dream about the seven years of famine, but that he could provide the answer to the problem of how to feed the people during that time. This Pharaoh was wiser than the one Moses and Aaron confronted. This Pharaoh was astounded by Joseph's great wisdom. In his systematic planning for storage of grain during the prophesied seven good years Joseph spoke wisdom for the infrastructure of the whole nation. Ultimately, all the surrounding nations came to Joseph for the grain he had stored.

Through Joseph we see what the Body of Christ is going to look like as it is raised up to govern with heavenly wisdom. When the Body of Christ is "purified, made spotless and refined" and functions as God intends, people will be hungry for true grain—the Word of God. The whole world will come to the Body of Christ for answers to the mess that has overtaken the earth. This is the "billion-soul harvest" as prophesied by prophet Bob

Jones. This worldwide harvest is the result of the massive revival of people coming for the "seed," the Word of God, the revelation of Yeshua.

# ABOUT ADAM F. THOMPSON

ADAM HAS A REMARKABLE GRACE TO INTERPRET DREAMS, RELEASE words of knowledge and operate in the prophetic. Supernatural signs and manifestations regularly accompany his ministry as he desires to see Jesus "magnified" through the moving of the Holy Spirit. He has ministered extensively in Pakistan, India, Africa, Indonesia, Papua New Guinea, Malaysia and the Philippines in crusades, feeding programs and pastors conferences. He is co-author of *Divinity Code* and author of *The Supernatural Man* and *Living from Heaven*. Adam operates itinerantly through his ministry Voice of Fire: www.voiceoffireministries.org.

# CONVERGENCE OF GLORY AND AUTHORITY

*Becca Greenwood*

THROUGHOUT HISTORY THE LORD HAS MOVED IN HIS PRO-
phetic times and seasons. He established the Hebrew calendar in
which each century, decade, and year is depicted by a Hebrew character
signifying prophetic insight. It is His divine design that we walk in timing with this prophetic wisdom to empower us with Kingdom vision: *"And
of the children of Issachar, which were men that had understanding of the
times, to know what Israel ought to do"* (1 Chron. 12:32 KJV). In alignment with this calendar we are in the year 5779. The significance of 70 is
depicted by the Hebrew symbol *ayin*. It is represented by an eye, which
means we are able to see and perceive what He is speaking. The number

nine is symbolized by the Hebrew character *tet*, resembling the appearance of a snake and at the same time a womb that is preparing to birth. The number nine signifies finality and judgment; it is used to define the perfect movement of God. We are also in the year 2019. Nineteen signifies a start and a finish—to maneuver in a starting of a new work with the anointing to carry it through to completion. Therefore, this year brings the prophetic realization that we are in a season graced with the increase to perceive and see the warfare tactics of the enemy exposed and defeated while giving birth to the new move of revelation, manifestation of the glory, and authority of the Lord.

He has also made available the filling, fire, and empowerment of the Holy Spirit through whom we are now able to see, perceive, and hear the strategic prophetic significance of the times we are in.

> On the day Pentecost was being fulfilled, all the disciples were gathered in one place. Suddenly they heard the sound of a violent blast of the wind rushing into the house from out of the heavenly realm. ...Then all at once a pillar of fire appeared before their eyes. It separated into tongues of fire that engulfed each one of them. They were all filled and equipped with the Holy Spirit and were inspired...empowered by the Spirit to speak in languages they had never learned! (Acts 2:1-4, TPT)

As I scribe this word I hear the Lord speaking:

"It is a time of a new outpouring of the oil, fire, and wine of My Spirit and presence, which will burn a passion of surrender. Waves of glory of My Father's heart of love will capture and envelop many. There will be shakings that occur, not just one and not just two, but shakings. The shakings will cause impurities to surface, repentance to occur, and an awakening to humility, holiness, and glory. This move of My Spirit will occur at an accelerated rate. *"The entire universe is standing on tiptoe, yearning to see the unveiling of God's glorious sons and daughters!"* (Rom. 8:19 TPT). It is a time of empowerment in faith to see signs and wonders and a sharpening multiplication in the gifts. I am breathing My breath of life on the awareness that My glory is an inheritance promise of Kingdom DNA. Out-of-the-box creative and strategic anointing will birth the new. It's a time of divine alignment, a manifestation of glory to birth Kingdom plans in authoritative inspiration and truth. There are specific warfare battles assigned for this time. Giants and strongholds will fall, and lands and spheres of inheritance and destiny possessed. The sharpened eagle vision, the ability to see the hidden prey is now. See now from My Kingdom perspective and receive strategies to overtake the giants of the past and possess that which has been promised. My Body is moving from the season of influence to Kingdom authority. The time of the greatest move of My Spirit is near."

## AWAKEN MY GLORY!

*Awake, my glory!* (Psalm 57:8)

*Arise, shine; for you light has come, and the glory of the Lord has risen upon you* (Isaiah 60:1).

The Hebrew word for "glory" is *kabod*. It means splendor, honor, wealth, manifestation of power, glorious presence, reward, glory in the inner person, ruler, men of high rank, and one who governs (Strong's #H3519). As David cried out to come up to a higher place of awakening to advance and see victory, this is a season when a cry is arising and the glory within is being awakened. His Spirit is hovering over individuals, corporate gatherings, businesses, governments, regions, and nations with the creative power to birth a fire and glory manifestation of the new era. *"The earth will be filled with the knowledge of the glory of the Lord"* (Hab. 2:14).

Your manifestation is in proportion to your revelation. Surrender to Him to gain more of Him. This is the year of face-to-face glory encounters with Him. In this place, life will come out of barrenness. Joy will come out of grief and despair. We will let go of those things that are slowing us down. We will see and know that in His glory everything is manifest that we need. We are moving from settling for the anointing to crossing the finish line of encountering the glory. A truth renewal is unfolding that His glory sustains and activates victory. To slay the giants, expose and defeat the enemy's strategies, and dethrone ancient principalities the glory is maturing within the Ekklesia—His legislative Body of believers.

> *And this truth of who I am will be the bedrock foundation on which I will build my church—my legislative assembly, and the power of death will not be able to overpower it!* (Matthew 16:18 TPT)

## The Lion of Judah Is Roaring!

> *Suddenly they heard the sound of a violent blast of wind rushing into the house from out of the heavenly realm. The roar of the wind was so overpowering it was all anyone could bear!* (Acts 2:2 TPT)

The translation for *sound* is blast of the trumpet, good report, roar like the waves of the ocean, and roar like a lion. In this season it is important to understand the significance of sound. The Holy Spirit has gone into the deepest part of each of us that can respond to Him, transforming from the inside out. He is renewing us to the invitation of the fullness of transformation that occurs from glory to glory. He is depositing in and releasing through us a distinct transformational sound. This roar of the lion is likened to the roar of the Lion of Judah. That sound and authority of His roar that has been deposited in us is being called forth and released. A roar of breakthrough, justice, truth, fire, glory, and victory. A bold roar to shift spiritual atmospheres and to break barriers of darkness.

A sound in praise and worship enveloped in prophetic intercession and birthed in His presence is going to another level for the pure in heart. From this place we will see God's perspectives, seeing others and situations with His eyes in a way we've not seen before. It is the hour for seers, hearers, intercessors, and believers to receive revelation that empowers to have great effect.

## RECEIVE STRATEGIES TO ADVANCE

It's time to receive Kingdom vision. We are encountering transition on many fronts. In the Spirit, I have seen whirlwinds that seem to bring storms. Within the churning winds creating the funnel cycle are the words hope and faith. The winds are blowing across our lives, cities, and nations. For some it is personal, for some corporate. It is being seen nationally and internationally. I inquired, and He revealed insight. It is a season when the winds will blow. Some will feel uncertain, unsafe. These are not winds for destruction in the natural. They are spiritual winds, winds of the Lord, causing a confrontation in the spirit realm and a shifting of spiritual atmospheres. In the midst of the whirlwinds, we are being invited into a season of transition—to embrace hope and faith as we cross over and possess anointing and strategies to advance for the days ahead.

Of these whirlwinds being revealed beginning in June 2018, three were blowing across Washington, DC. They will affect government and the judicial system. Whirlwinds were blowing across Maryland. I saw winds above Arizona, Indiana, Texas, Kansas, Florida, Georgia, Arkansas, the plains of Colorado, North Carolina, and South Carolina, and many sweeping across cities and regions in our nation. As these spiritual winds blow in this tumultuous time they will produce and bear fruit of faith, hope, righteousness, truth, and justice. The Lord is causing a shifting and sifting to be at play. The season of stretching and uncertainty is inviting us into abandoned and surrendered encounters, abiding in Him. To see, hear, and receive from Him a renewing of our minds. A newfound strength and fiery passion leading to victory!

## The Crossing Over Road

I see spiritually many are journeying down the familiar path always taken. He is causing a new road called the "crossing over road"—an intersection of the new road that is ahead. Here are action steps of wisdom:

1. Do not get stuck in transition or challenge of past failures.

2. Shake it off!

   - Shake off the dust of the past that has caused weariness.

   - Shake off the rehearsing of all that didn't go right.

3. Shut out voices that will speak contrary to His direction. Listen to His voice of faith. This is a season to be with those whose faith can become your faith to cross over.

4. He is speaking how to go a new way even in a season of contradiction. Partner with Him in your redefining and starting over moment.

5. Stop being afraid of what could go wrong and start being excited about what could go right.

6. Pioneers, intercessors, warriors, believers set your gaze on Him for strategies and assignments—move with Him.

7. Wisdom is being released concerning relationships. Relate/align with those who have wisdom and celebrate who you are in all seasons, from transition through your triumph and victories. Choose wisely. Honor unlocks glory.

This "crossing over road" is bringing nations into an intersection of the new road of realignment. The clash of the kingdoms, the clashing of swords, will continue in our nation. It is not about a political party, but a battle of light and dark. I see this occurring through 2019 and into 2020. Don't shrink back! If we continue to pray and take action the winds and clashing will bring victory. Mexico, hear the Word of the Lord, "The corruption that has gripped you in bondage will be shaken to its core. And the wind of spiritual encounter will uproot the ancient stronghold of death and idolatry in the land." China, your game of manipulation control is being exposed. To the spiritual army in China, now is the time to arise to see the grip of persecution broken or it will increase in days ahead. Russia, the season of playing to both sides will cause certain nations to arise and confront. Israel, a harvest of souls and glory move of the Spirit is upon you. I continue to see the cities of Atlanta and Nashville. The move of the Lord will cause that which has been prophesied to birth. Dallas, the season of glory and transformation is on the horizon. Chicago, the grip of corrupt structures of greed, violence, and death is shaking. The apostolic and prophetic is set in place to see the schemes of control defeated.

I am seeing a six-year period of time where the legalization of abortion will continue to be unraveled/undone. State by state. Case by case. Justice by justice. New legislation is coming.

## Sound of Strategists Arising!

Kingdom strategists are arising. Their calling is not an event-focused mindset. Relational and strategic alliances are being forged for transformation. Some have sat on the sidelines waiting for the perfect opportunity.

The Lord is saying, "Be the pioneer to blaze a glory trail and birth the new that I am revealing to you."

> *There is a divine mystery—a secret surprise that has been concealed from the world for generations, but now it's being revealed, unfolded and manifested for every holy believer to experience. Living within you is the Christ who floods you with the expectation of glory! This mystery of Christ, embedded within us, becomes a heavenly treasure chest of hope filled with the riches of glory for his people, and God wants everyone to know it!* (Colossians 1:26-27 TPT)

He's imparting a passion cry: "Lord, it's about You and Your Kingdom." Say yes! Pioneers who have paid the price are emerging to be a reconciling force. They will clear the path, blaze the trail, and lead the way.

## Be Ready!

Intercessors, be ready to roll! It's time for the giant slayers! Davids, arise! It's time for the city and nation deliverers to get your marching orders and advance. Moseses, arise! It is time to get Kingdom of God "out of the box" glory-birthed strategies. Joshuas, Josephs, Daniels, Esthers, Deborahs—it's time to possess gates of influence. Governmental intercessors arise, advance. We are in a now moment. Much is at stake. As we advance in His strategies, we move from defense to offense and thwart the schemes of the enemy. We must strategize and intercede in His Kingdom assignments to usher in the harvest that is on the horizon.

## Strategies for Victory!

Strategies for victory are now concerning issues and lingering nuisances that you are pressing through and that have held you back. It is occurring personally, corporately, nationally, and internationally. Some have been asking, "What is this assignment of the enemy in my life or family blood-line that continues to hold me back? Lord, what is Your prayer strategy for our cities, regions, and nation?"

I heard the Lord say, "That snake in the grass, that demon of darkness that has kept himself hidden is now about to overplay his hand and expose himself. And you will discern and see this serpent and his schemes and secure a sudden and swift victory!" When you see this dark scheme for what it truly is, don't hesitate to take authority over it! That moment is not the time to remain silent or shrink back. The King is in the field on your behalf.

> *When Pharaoh says to you, Prove [your authority] by a miracle, then tell Aaron, Throw your rod down before Pharaoh, that it may become a serpent. So Moses and Aaron went to Pharaoh and did as the Lord had commanded; Aaron threw down his rod before Pharaoh and his servants, and it became a serpent. Then Pharaoh called for the wise men [skilled in magic and divination] and the sorcerers (wizards and jugglers). And they also, these magicians of Egypt, did similar things with their enchantments and secret arts. For they cast down every man his rod and they became serpents; but Aaron's rod swallowed up their rods* (Exodus 7:9-12 AMPC).

As the Lord supernaturally moved on behalf of Moses and Aaron when Pharaoh asked for a sign of proved authority, He is now releasing strategies to see occult and corrupt world systems and structures defeated. The Queen of Heaven's grip on corrupt and monetary structures and media is being exposed. The Deborahs are arising to cut off her hold. God's authority will swallow up the strategies of the enemy and the world. His authority trumps all powers. Angel armies are with us. There are more for us than against us.

## Women Arise

The season of minimizing and apologizing for the position as an influential woman is ending. It is the forerunning season for gender issues to be healed. The great divide that has been evident for thousands of years will begin to be healed in an unprecedented measure. An awakening of the Deborahs, Esthers, Lydias is occurring. The slumber is lifting from the weight of religious culture and many women will emerge to have great impact.

## Joy, Joy, Joy!

Allow joy into your life! In His presence He will restore joy. Your joy in Him will move you forward! His joy becomes your joy and strength! Joy will be found, restored, and re-fired in our personal lives, situations, and prayer assignments. What we believe and speak out becomes the prophecy by which we live out our lives. We are our own personal prophets! Prophesy in agreement with His plans and purposes. Allow His joy, truth, and love to fill the words of your mouth. Welcome His life, fire, glory, joy, and love to come to those dry places. Flesh, sinew, and life are forming on those dry, dead bones. *It is time for those lifeless and dry bones to receive resurrection life.*

# ABOUT REBECCA GREENWOOD

REBECCA GREENWOOD CO-FOUNDED CHRISTIAN HARVEST International, which ministers to the nations through prophetic intercession, transformational spiritual warfare prayer, and teaching of the word of God. Over the past 24 years, she has participated and led in spiritual warfare prayer journeys to 34 countries in which measurable transformations have been realized. Rebecca and her husband Greg reside in Colorado Springs, CO and they have three beautiful daughters.

# THE SWORD OF ELISHA

*Rich Vera*

And he [Elijah] said, "I have been very zealous for the Lord God of hosts; because the children of Israel have forsaken Your covenant, torn down Your altars, and killed Your prophets with the sword. I alone am left; and they seek to take my life."

Then the Lord said to him: "Go, return on your way to the Wilderness of Damascus; and when you arrive, anoint Hazael as king over Syria. Also you shall anoint Jehu the son of Nimshi as king over Israel. And Elisha the son of Shaphat of Abel Meholah you shall anoint as prophet in your place. It shall be that whoever escapes the sword of Hazael, Jehu will kill; and whoever escapes the sword of Jehu, Elisha will kill.

—1 KINGS 19:14-17 NKJV

WE ARE LIVING IN A VERY IMPORTANT TIME IN CHURCH AND world history. There is a cry for the new; for voices with fresh sound and new demonstration; for true spiritual transformation over nations, territories, cities, churches, and our own personal lives. In this new season God is answering our cries. The passing of the baton is taking place now—the rising up of a new generation of anointed and appointed leaders who will be warriors and giant killers, the generation that was prophesied in Malachi 4:2-6:

> *"But to you who fear My name the Sun of Righteousness shall arise with healing in His wings; and you shall go out and grow fat like stall-fed calves. You shall trample the wicked, for they shall be ashes under the soles of your feet on the day that I do this," says the Lord of hosts. "Remember the Law of Moses, My servant, which I commanded him in Horeb for all Israel, with the statutes and judgments. Behold, I will send you Elijah the prophet before the coming of the great and dreadful day of the Lord. And he will turn the hearts of the fathers to the children, and the hearts of the children to their fathers"* (NKJV).

Elijah represents the old guard, anointed and raised by God, zealous for the Lord and His work, but with a selfish heart, unwilling to father the next generation, believing only they have been anointed!

Elisha represents the *new* generation that walks in the double portion—those who have seen the Elijahs of our time and have learned and received from them but also have their own experience and encounter with God, ready to not commit the mistakes of the older generation, and daring enough to fly higher!

With this new generation God will move in unusual ways, demonstrating His healing power by the brightness of His presence in them, not only to heal bodies but cities, territories, and nations. A higher dimension we have never seen is about to come on the scene. They speak different, walk different; they are not afraid of confrontation nor attacks; they can never be destroyed nor stopped; and those who dig for their graves shall fall into them themselves.

Jehovah is with them in *mighty power*. They will speak and heaven will listen; they will walk and territories will tremble at their presence with authority and true power over demons, principalities, and Satan.

I am talking about the arrival of *the prophets*.

When I speak about fathering I am not talking about the American traditional way of fathering. To *father* means to raise up, to invest, to train, to correct, and to stand by those who are sons, in good and bad times, until they have fully matured and become carriers of the legacy and spirit of the fathers.

As Elijah was coming to an end of his earthly ministry and unable to defeat Jezebel, the Lord gave him specific instructions, and he was commanded to raise up new leaders.

Let me explain what I see in the Spirit.

The Body of Christ has what I call three types of leadership functioning today:

## AHAZIAH

Ahaziah was a king of Judah, and it is said that he was a descendant of Omri who was known as the wickedest king to rule. Ahaziah was also the nephew of Ahab and the first Judahite king to be descended from both the house of David and the house of Omri.

Influenced by his mother Athaliah, sister of Ahab, he introduced *forms of worship* that offended the Yahwistic party.

Ahaziah's advisors were members of his own family who would tell him what he wanted to hear, eventually leading to his death.

This represents the leadership that, though gifted, still carries a mixed spirit and was never circumcised at the heart (see Rom. 2:25-29). They never allowed God's process of purging and inner transformation.

Generational curses are still attached to them, yet they have gifts with the anointing those gifts carry. They stand before people and do their thing, helping some, but with no power over the spirit and demonic world and no real encounter with God. They have not spent time in His presence to be transformed and to receive true *power*.

## JEHU

Jehu was a commander in the army of Ahab (see 2 Kings 9). His name means "Yahweh is He"—a man with a heart to stand for God with a God-given task and the heart of a reformer. He obliterated the house of Ahab, along with the worship of Baal that pervaded Israel at the time.

God also chose Jehu to be the king of Israel. After he was anointed king, Jehu made haste to Jezreel and killed two of Ahab's sons—Joram, king of northern Israel, and Ahaziah, king of Judah (see 2 Kings 9:14-29). Jehu then proceeded to Jezebel's palace in Jezreel, where the queen stood watching for him at her window. At Jehu's command, eunuchs surrounding Jezebel threw her down from the window. Jezebel's blood splattered over the pavement, and, just as had occurred to Ahab, her blood was licked up by the dogs and her body eaten (see 2 Kings 9:30-37; 1 Kings 21:20-26; 22:37-38).

Jehu left no man standing who was in alliance with King Ahab, as God had commanded long before through Elijah. Entering the temple of Baal, Jehu slaughtered all the priests of Baal and destroyed the temple and its sacred stone, thus eradicating Baal worship in Israel (see 2 Kings 10:23-28).

The Lord blessed Jehu for his obedience, granting him a dynasty that would last to the fourth generation (see 2 Kings 10:30). However, because Jehu continued to hold on to the idolatrous worship of King Jeroboam (see 2 Kings 10:29; God began to reduce the size of Israel, gradually giving them over to the power of Hazael of Syria (see 2 Kings 10:32-33).

Jehu represents the leadership that has a call from God and they have been anointed for a task. They carry their function and God uses them; however, they compromise and walk in the fear of man, trying to please man, and are unwilling to take a stand because they fear rejection or persecution and have put their guard down. Eventually their call weakens and they lose the favor of God.

## ELISHA

A prophet with a double portion who walked in power and no compromise, he could not be bought with money or gifts. He walked in supernatural power as a prophet who was fearless with miracle power in his hands.

Elisha represents the new generation of *power prophets* who are coming to the nations. What the previous generations have not been able to accomplish and what the current leadership can't overcome, *the Elisha company* will destroy.

Notice the Bible says *the sword of Elisha*, yet he never carried a sword in his hands. Only in his *mouth*—to declare and to speak on behalf of heaven and see heaven move on their behalf.

This *Elisha company* will destroy demonic strongholds in nations and people, they will deliver people by just speaking by the Spirit over them, and they will accomplish in one generation what many previous could not! They will be giant killers, dragon slayers, Jezebel destroyers. They won't be able to be destroyed nor stopped as God will be with them in power. They will restore the credibility of God's name to the nations and shock many with acts of power. Entire regions will come into revival by this *prophetic company* with power to even affect government and society.

The sword of Elisha carries fire and demons flee as they open their mouth. They will make the sinner turn, the religious growl, and the compromiser tremble.

Get ready; this company is coming in this season. It will carry an anointing and edge like we have never seen before. That company is here *now*.

# ABOUT RICH VERA

RICH VERA TRAVELS THE WORLD SPEAKING IN CHURCHES, AND holding massive miracle rallies, where thousands of people gather to experience the Presence and touch of God. Catholics and people from all faiths gather by the thousands to experience the ministry of the Holy Spirit.

# Cyber Evangelism and Discipleship: Bringing in the Billion-Soul Harvest

*Patricia King*

A NUMBER OF SEASONED PROPHETS OVER THE LAST 20 YEARS have been prophesying a billion-soul harvest that will come in with one sweep of the sickle.

In 2006 when I was in a conversation with Prophet Bob Jones regarding the billion-soul harvest, he said, "Watch 2020. Prepare for 2020. It's going to peak."

Although we understand prophetically that this great billion-soul harvest is promised and indeed will swell over the next couple of years, we need to also realize that it has actually already begun! Souls are being saved en masse even at this moment, even as you are reading this chapter.

Reports of mass crusades with hundreds of thousands and even millions in attendance with masses coming to Christ are not unusual in some nations, but this harvest is not just for "some nations"—it is for all!

John 4:35 is a *rhema and kairos* word[1] for the Church in this hour as Jesus reveals that the harvest fields are ripe and ready now! Now is the time to reap.

> *Do you not say, "There are still four months and then comes the harvest"? Behold, I say to you, lift up your eyes and look at the fields, for they are already white for harvest!* (John 4:35 NKJV)

## New Wineskins for the Harvest

Paul taught that there were many ways to win people's hearts to Christ, and he was willing to do whatever it took through righteous means to bring them the revelation of the gospel.

> *For though I am free from all men, I have made myself a servant to all, that I might win the more; and to the Jews I became as a Jew, that I might win Jews; to those who are under the law, as under the law, that I might win those who are under the law; to those who are without law, as without law (not being without law toward God, but under law toward Christ), that I might win those who are without law; to the weak I became as weak, that I might win the weak. I have become all things to all men, **that I might by all means save some.** Now this I do for the gospel's sake, that I may be partaker of it with you* (1 Corinthians 9:19-23 NKJV).

God is using many means to win souls through His people, and all of these means will win some. There is to be no judgment concerning the way another believer is winning souls to Christ if it is righteous. I will at times hear criticism toward those who are called to crusade evangelism from leaders who believe church planting is the best way to reach the lost. I sometimes hear criticism and even mockery from the Body regarding those who are engaging in prophetic evangelism on the streets or in extreme venues such as psychic fairs and porn conventions. Others criticize seeker-friendly outreaches and perspectives. We must be willing to embrace each other as we are winning souls for Christ. Not everyone will have the same call or the same conviction, but let's be committed to bringing in the harvest together and be open to new ways to reach them.

## CYBER EVANGELISM AND DISCIPLESHIP: A NEW WINESKIN

Jesus taught His disciples regarding the flexibility required for a fresh move of the Spirit.

> *No one puts new wine into old wineskins; otherwise the wine will burst the skins, and the wine is lost and the skins as well; but one puts new wine into fresh wineskins* (Mark 2:22).

Historically, we have discovered that many do not adapt quickly to change or to new ways of doing things, but it is imperative that we discern the times and that we are willing to do things differently in this hour.

Throughout Church history we see those who embraced the previous move often become the strongest resistance to the new move. We need to remain open to the Spirit especially during the harvest in order to bring it in without losing even one.

Social media through the Internet is one of the significant ways God is going to use His Body to reach the lost in this hour. We can reach thousands and even millions with one click.

Let's look at a scripture through prophetic eyes. The Book of Revelation is a challenging book to interpret at the best of times, and it can be interpreted on multiple levels. I want to take prophetic license with you to reveal something the Lord has shown me regarding the billion-soul harvest and the cyber realm.

When you unpack a Spirit-inspired scripture with prophetic license, you must make sure that there is nothing in the prophetic revelation that would be contrary to the nature, character, and whole counsel of God. With that presupposition, I present the following.

Let's look at Revelation 14:6:

> *And I saw another **angel** flying in **midheaven**, having an eternal gospel to preach to those who live on the earth, and to every nation and tribe and tongue and people.*

The word, *angel* in this passage is not the same Greek word that is used in Hebrews 1:14 to describe angels (*pneuma*) but rather it is a Greek word (*aggelos*) meaning "messenger."

The word *midheaven* (Greek, *mesouranēma*) does not refer to God's place of abode in the third heaven, but rather to the natural heavens. In John's day they did not have the Internet, although it was in God's plan. The "midheaven" could easily be prophetically applied to the cyber-heaven realm.

We see in this verse that the eternal gospel was being preached by the "angel" (messenger: the Church) in "midheaven" (cyber-heaven) reaching those who live on the earth, and to every nation and tribe and tongue and people. Never before in Church history have we been able to reach every nation, tribe, and tongue as we are able to today. Often with social media posts you can easily reach over 120 nations with one post and thousands and even millions of views.

Our ministry does a lot of work in the slums of Cambodia. They are very poor, but there are still many with smartphones and those with computer and the Internet. One day, I was walking through a village and someone had a computer with a video being viewed by many in the village. Even in some of the most remote and poorest places in the world, they have access to the Internet.

Let's look now at Revelation 14:14:

> *Then I looked, and behold, a white **cloud**, and sitting on the **cloud** was one like a son of man, having a golden crown on His head and a sharp sickle in His hand.*

Today, we are very familiar with the word *cloud* as it is a household word around the globe when it comes to the Internet. In John's day he would not have had understanding concerning this. You will notice, however, that *Jesus* was *sitting on the cloud!* The golden crown on His head speaks of His kingly authority and the sharp sickle in His hand was a harvesting tool in that day.

I have heard many believers complain about the Internet as it exports so much evil (i.e. pornography, corruption, foul language, dark web, etc.) but God wants us to take ownership and rule over "the cloud"! He wants the cloud for His glory! He wants His people to use it as an instrument to bring in the harvest.

> *And **another angel** came out of the temple, crying out with a loud voice to Him who sat on **the cloud**, "Put in your sickle and reap, for **the hour to reap has come**, because the harvest of the earth is ripe"* (Revelation 14:15).

We see in this scripture that there was a God-appointed *kairos* time for the harvest of the earth to be reaped. It is interesting that another angel (messenger) cried from the temple. We are the temple of the Holy Spirit. This could speak of the groanings of God's people in intercession that releases a *kairos* prophetic cry unto the Lord to put in His sickle. The Lord is in partnership with His Church. We have the keys. We are His agents in the earth to release His hand. He confirmed this as He taught His disciples:

> *I will give you the keys of the kingdom of heaven; and whatever you bind on earth shall have been bound in heaven, and whatever you loose on earth shall have been loosed in heaven* (Matthew 16:19).

In Isaiah, God invites us to ask Him concerning the future of His sons and then to command the works of His hands.

> *Thus saith the Lord, the Holy One of Israel, and his Maker, Ask me of things to come concerning my sons, and concerning the work of my hands command ye me* (Isaiah 45:11 KJV).

God's people will begin to cry out for the lost in this hour as never before. These groanings will be responded to by the Lord Himself.

We see in Revelation 14:16, "*Then He who sat on the cloud swung His sickle over the earth, and the earth was reaped.*" When Jesus swings His sickle, so also does His Church as we are His Body and He does nothing in the earth independently of us.

## Find the Need

In John 4 we read the story about Jesus meeting the Samaritan woman at the well. It is a beautiful story of how He led her into truth. One of the keys is that He found her need and ministered into the situation. She was a woman who had many questions, and Jesus revealed Himself to her.

Today there are many in the world with severe and urgent needs. We, the Church, have the answers for them. As a ministry, the first video that we posted online for the lost was regarding depression. Many in the world suffer from it—we discovered the need. I shared my own testimony and invited them to receive Jesus into their hearts. I also offered them a mini-webinar on how to overcome depression and a website we produced that hosts over 20 follow-up discipleship videos. We posted the testimony on social media and then paid for target marketing through social media portals to those who are depressed. As a result multiple thousands heard the gospel and had their very need targeted with the truth that would set them free.

It is easy for every church to host similar testimonies that meet needs and develop sites to disciple new believers. It is not only important to bring in the harvest but also to disciple new believers. We are anointed and appointed to make disciples of the nations.

The Lord says that, "In this hour, the Internet will be used as a powerful tool for evangelism and also for discipleship. I am ready to swing My sickle. Are you ready?"

> *And Jesus came up and spoke to them, saying, "All authority has been given to Me in heaven and on earth. Go therefore and make disciples of all the nations, baptizing them in the name of the Father and the Son and the Holy Spirit, teaching them to observe all that I commanded you; and lo, I am with you always, even to the end of the age"* (Matthew 28:18-20).

I was in an evangelism crusade in an unreached area of India in 2017. Over 35,000 souls came to know Jesus as Savior in a three-day event after hearing the gospel for the first time ever. There was one small full gospel church in the area who was involved with hosting the event. How were they to disciple such a harvest? If there was an Internet site the new believers could have accessed in their own language and according to their own culture, many of them could have received the foundations they needed to begin their journey of faith in Christ.

Obviously one on one is the best for quality discipleship, but in this great season of harvest we might not be able to reach them all easily with the manpower we have on hand. This is why the Lord is highlighting this great tool of cyber-discipleship. Our ministry's discipleship videos include introductory teachings on the Father's heart, how to pray, how to read the Word, etc., and we also offer a new believers Facebook page where we have "cyber-pastors" manning it.

Many ministries are already using the Internet to air their services, teachings, and conferences, and many are also using the Internet for evangelism outreach and discipleship. But in this hour, it is time for all to utilize the Internet.

The days in which we are living are exciting times. God has put powerful tools in our hands. Let's embrace the *cloud* and bring Him great glory!

## Note

1.  *Rhema* is a Greek word for "Word"—a Holy Spirit quickened word. Strong's Concordance #G4487 defines *rhema* as "that which is or has been uttered by the living voice, thing spoken, word." *Kairos* is a "God-appointed time." Strong's Concordance #G2540 defines *kairos* as "a fixed and definite time, the time when things are brought to crisis, the decisive epoch waited for."

# About Patricia King

Patricia King is a respected apostolic minister of the gospel, successful business owner, and an inventive entrepreneur. She is an accomplished itinerant speaker, author, television host, media producer, and ministry network overseer who has given her life fully to Jesus Christ and to His Kingdom's advancement in the earth. She is the founder of Patricia King Ministries and co-founder of XPmedia.com.

# THE AWAKENING CHURCH OF 2019

*Germaine Griffin Copeland*

In the year 2017, *Prayers That Avail Much for the Nations* was published, and some questioned why we should pray for other nations when our own nation is in turmoil. We ask ourselves does John 3:16 really mean *all* the world? Are we to take the Bible literally and offer our bodies a living sacrifice that we might become "houses" of prayer for *all* nations? (See Isaiah 56:7 NLT.)

Could 2019 be the year the Church cries out, "Consecrate me now to Thy service, Lord, by Thy power of grace divine...let my will be lost in Thine?"[1] May this be the year our minds grasp the meaning of First Corinthians 2:16 and our prayers issue from the very Throne Room of God.

*For "who has known the mind of the Lord that he may instruct Him?" But we have the mind of Christ* (1 Corinthians 2:16 NKJV).

Then I began working on *Prayers That Avail Much for America*—a book of prayers published in 2018. Will the prayers of the saints prepare the pathway from heaven to earth and experience a great spiritual awakening? Might this be the year of the manifestation of the glorious Church? (See Ephesians 5:27.) Many believers are praying from both these publications, and other prayer movements have grown exponentially. Prayer, once again, is the order of the day.

We assumed our responsibility, we volunteered to rebuild the walls of salvation for our nation and refuse to come down. We are praying "Prayers of Destiny," "Prayers of Promise" and "Prayers of Repentance."[2] With each passing day we continue to stand against the unseen enemy whose time is drawing short.

The shadow of fear whispers, "Did Jesus really say upon this rock I will build My Church and the gates of hell will not prevail against it? (See Matthew 16:18.) All you have to do is look at the news of the day to know that can't possibly be true." With eyes wide open we declare confidently it is written: Jesus is the way, the Truth, and the Life (see John 14:6), and He is building His Church.

In the last few years, our faith grew as the waves roared and the deep, tumultuous waters threatened to take us under. All the time Jesus is walking toward us extending a simple invitation: "Come." (Taking a deep breath I step out of the boat, and look to our Redeemer—the Savior of the world. Am I ready to walk on the wild and stormy water?) Our faith grew as looming, unsurmountable mountains suddenly appeared. Our faith grew as the gale winds blew and the skies grew dark with ominous clouds, clamorous thundering, and fierce lightening. Today, we are a people *"strong in the Lord and the power of His might"* (Eph. 6:10 NKJV). Will we continue to look to Jesus, our soon-coming King?

In the New Year I see the Church awakening from slumber. The Church of 2019 will no longer be a church based on traditions; our prayers will no longer issue from our diverse personal interpretations and agendas. A transformation is happening; we are in the middle of something miraculous. Is it true? We were birthed on the Day of Pentecost to be the triumphant, glorious Church. We are awake, we have risen from the dead, and Christ has given us light in a time of great darkness. The Scripture says, "Arise, shine; for your light has come! And the glory of the Lord is risen upon you" (Isa. 60:1 NKJV). We are the Awakening Church of 2019!

The Church is returning to her first love, remembering from where we have fallen. We humbly bow before the Father and repent for devising our own plans and making ministry about "the arm of flesh." Too often we followed after a man rather than the Most High God who loves us with an everlasting, unconditional love. Here we are, looking to Jesus who is the Author and Finisher of our faith, enjoying sweet fellowship with Him. The Holy Spirit is no longer the forgotten God! The wind of the Holy Spirit is sweeping into sanctuaries, and the Church of 2019 will experience revival and transformation that overflows outside the upper rooms into the highways and byways. Signs and wonders are on the horizon.

This is the year we begin to witness the multitudes of people searching for the Light. Sex traffickers, Satan worshipers, drug dealers, pedophiles, prostitutes will look to the Church for love, healing, and answers. A great awakening has begun and will grow to tsunami proportions. People matter, and Jesus saves to the uttermost! (See Hebrews 7:25 NKJV.)

## PREPARING FOR HARVEST

*If I could speak all the languages of earth and of angels, but didn't love others, I would only be a noisy gong or a clanging cymbal. If I had the gift of prophecy, and if I understood all of God's secret plans and possessed all knowledge, and if I had such faith that I could move mountains, but didn't love others, I would be nothing. If I gave everything I have to the poor and even sacrificed my body, I could boast about it; but if I didn't love others, I would have gained nothing* (1 Corinthians 13:1-3 NLT).

In today's world we see the words of Jesus in Matthew 24 unfolding across the United States of America and around the world. Spiritual deception is invading the Church; there are wars, rumors of wars; racial and ethnic conflict is increasing; earthquakes, tornadoes, persecution of Christians is on the rise. Let us not hesitate to prepare for the great awakening. As God's co-laborers, it is time to lay aside our old wineskins and *"cleanse ourselves from everything that can defile our body or spirit. And let us work toward complete holiness because we fear God"* (2 Cor. 7:1 NLT).

This vision for 2019 overwhelms me and I wish I could tell you with certainty that this will be the year of the great awakening when multitudes are coming into the Kingdom of Heaven. With all my heart I want to tell you with certainty that this will be the year when the Church will choose to set her heart on things above, where Christ is seated at the right hand of God (see Col. 3:1). Will this be the year when we believe that there abides faith, hope, and love, and the greatest of these is love? (See First Corinthians 13:13.) Will this be the year we are known as His disciples by our love for one another? (See John 13:34-35.) I can tell you with certainty this is the will of the Father. The choice is ours.

Will we individually take the necessary time out of the busyness of life to know God intimately? I pray that we will cry out from the depths of our being:

*That I may know Him and the power of His resurrection, and the fellowship of His sufferings, being conformed to His death, if, by any means, I may attain to the resurrection from the dead* (Philippians 3:10-11 NKJV).

There is no way that Christians, in a private capacity, can do so much to promote the work of God and advance the kingdom of Christ as by prayer.

—Jonathan Edwards

How are you praying for believers who disagree with your interpretation of the Scriptures? How do you pray for those who disagree with you politically? God "*has delivered us from the power of darkness and conveyed us into the kingdom of the Son of His love, in whom we have redemption through His blood, the forgiveness of sins*" (Col. 1:13-14 NKJV). In his epistles the apostle Paul left us examples of how to pray for one another. Will we pray for others because we are born of love or pray for others because our lives would be easier if they would change? The choice is ours!

Will 2019 be the year when diverse cultures no longer judge one another for the sins of our ancestors? Are we ready to erase the records of being wronged? I am praying that we know the reality of being "in Him," that we will choose to trust God's love that He has poured out into our hearts by the Holy Ghost and see one another with His eyes, truly loving one another. We are no longer clinging to our fears, but we are walking in the light of God's love. We know that we have passed from death to life because we love one another (see 1 John 3:14).

*This is the message which we have heard from Him and declare to you, that God is light and in Him is no darkness at all. If we say that we have fellowship with Him, and walk in darkness, we lie and do not practice the truth. But if we walk in the light as He is in the light, we have fellowship with one another, and the blood of Jesus Christ His Son cleanses us from all sin* (1 John 1:5-7 NKJV).

Will this be the year when our will is lost in His will, when our prayers flow from our identity "in Christ" rather than this earthly identity? I am praying and believing that this will be the year when we see the fulfillment—at least the beginning of the fulfillment—of the prayer Jesus prayed. We will identify with this One who said, "*I in them, and You in Me; that they may be made perfect in one, and that the world may know that You have sent Me, and have loved them as You have loved Me*" (John 17:23 NKJV).

With all my heart I pray this will be the year we, the Body of Christ, return to our first love. Let this be the year when the followers of Jesus will be known by our love for one another. Then we shall be world-changers, kings and priests who are seated in Christ "*far above any ruler or authority or power or leader or anything else—not only in this world but also in the world to come*" (Eph. 1:21 NLT).

In 2019 the glorious Church is open and ready for all who will come. A young man walked into the church carrying his Quran, wearing a tank top so everyone could see his many tattoos. It did not take long to know that he was uneducated and had lived on the streets of downtown Atlanta, Georgia. God sent him and exposed my prejudice. No matter how I tried to avoid him, he would find me and give me a hug. He continued to come to our church, and I learned to hug him back. Even as I write the memories of a special day, my heart overflows with thanksgiving. He was born again, and later I would understand that he was looking for a mother's love— even greater than that, he discovered the Father's unconditional love. Let's remember from where we have come and prepare ourselves for the end-time harvest of a world who is lost without God. Are we prepared? May the Father cause His perfect love in us to drive all our fears out of doors.

The choice is ours! May we choose wisely.

*And this gospel of the kingdom will be preached in all the world as a witness to all the nations, and then the end will come* (Matthew 24:14 NKJV).

There's a great day coming!

*After these things I looked, and behold, a great multitude which no one could number, of all nations, tribes, peoples, and tongues, standing before the throne and before the Lamb, clothed with white robes, with palm branches in their hands, and crying out with a loud voice, saying, "Salvation belongs to our God who sits on the throne, and to the Lamb!"* (Revelation 7:9-10 NKJV).

## ENDNOTES

1. Fanny Crosby, "Nearer Blessed Lord," 1875, public domain.

2. *Prayers That Avail Much,* ©Copyright Germaine Copeland.

# About Germaine Griffin Copeland

Germaine Copeland is the author of the best-selling *Prayers That Avail Much* book series. Founder of Word Ministries, Germaine travels nationally and internationally conducting prayer schools, speaking at churches, conferences, and other groups. As she ministers, people are encouraged by her insight on praying effectively, experience emotional healing, and learn how prayer promotes personal change, making a difference in the spiritual climates within their spheres of influence. Germaine and her husband, Everette, have four adult children, 11 grandchildren and 11 great-grandchildren. They reside in Greensboro, Georgia.

# THE NINTH HOUR: FROM SURVIVAL TO REVIVAL!

*Jane Hamon*

GOD IS ALWAYS SPEAKING TO HIS PEOPLE, BUT AT SPECIAL TIMES of celebration and commemoration, prophets and prophetic people listen for His words that will focus us for this new season. As we enter the Roman calendar year 2019 and the Hebraic calendar year 5779 we are asking for clarity and understanding of God's purposes so that we can properly position ourselves to receive and cooperate with all that heaven desires to perform.

God's present word for a season will often connect to previous words from previous seasons. Prophetic words are like road signs confirming His path and direction as we journey forward. One sign might indicate that we are to keep proceeding on the previous route and that these are some markers of what to expect to see. Other words may indicate a turn or a change of direction, yet a continuation of the same journey. In the last several years God has spoken to me that we are in a time of *divine reversals*, both for individuals and for nations, that we are in a *tipping point* moment, and that we are in the time of the *prophet's reward*, to name a few. These words connect us to God's heart, plan, and reformation purposes in the earth.

This year as I prayed I heard the Lord say that this will be *a time of birthing* what we have been carrying and that *He is taking His people and our land from survival to revival!* We are in the 30th year of the birthing of the prophetic movement and it is time to see the prophet's reward (see Matt. 10:40-41), which is breakthrough, miracles, abundance, increase, and heaven fighting for us.

## DEFINING REVIVAL

It's important to know that the definition of *revival* is not just a series of outpourings or crusade meetings; it means "to bring back to life, consciousness, vigor, vitality, strength or a flourishing condition; a spiritual awakening; to quicken, restore, and renew hope and confidence; to activate or set things into motion; to make operative or valid again; to quicken or renew the mind; to recover from financial depression; to rejuvenate, reactivate, resuscitate and revitalize." Wow! Revival is for everyone—the lost, the prodigal, the brokenhearted, the one struggling through doubt and unbelief, the one in desperate need of a miracle, the revolutionary, and the reformer. We are coming out of survival into revival! Let's take a look at what that will mean for us in the coming year.

### Nine: Finishing One Cycle and Breaking into the New

The first important aspect to this new season is prophetically found in the end number for both the Roman and Hebraic years—the number nine. The number nine denotes the *finishing of a cycle* as we finish this decade with a sense of looking forward and not back. As we look to Scripture about the significance of how this number is used I believe there are several interesting and powerful keys that will enable us to unlock a surge of expectation, revelation, and transformation effective for our personal lives, the Church, and for our nation as well.

## Nine: A Fresh Manifestation of the Holy Spirit in the Life of the Believer

In Scripture we find that there are nine gifts of the Holy Spirit, nine fruits of the Holy Spirit, and nine Beatitudes given by Christ to align us to His heart for one another and for the earth. Paul declared:

> *And my speech and my preaching were not with persuasive words of human wisdom, but **in demonstration of the Spirit and of power**, that your faith should not be in the wisdom of men but in the power of God* (1 Corinthians 2:4-5 NKJV).

This is a time when we must be continuously filled with the Holy Spirit to fully accomplish His divine purpose. We must increase our time of praying in the Spirit and activating the gifts of the Holy Spirit to experience His fullness. We must also allow the development of the fruit of the Holy Spirit with the corresponding attitudes, which exemplify righteousness and set us free from confinement. Remember, gifts are given but fruit is grown. It will be imperative that we have Ephesians 1:17-18 operating in our lives as God releases the spirit of wisdom and revelation in us on new levels and with new requirements of function. When the Holy Spirit reveals Himself in new ways we will be set free from sin, from defeating habit patterns, and from limiting mindsets that hold us in survival. The Holy Spirit will break us out of survival and bring us into revival!

## A Birthing Season of Breakthrough

As a woman gives birth in the ninth month so will the church begin to birth the breakthroughs we have been carrying, releasing a time of fruitfulness, blessing, joy, fulfillment, and harvest. The ninth letter of the Hebraic alphabet is the letter *tet*. Scholars say it is associated with the picture of a pregnant woman (though honestly I can't always see the similarity!). A pregnant woman is said to be "expecting." I hear the challenge of the Holy Spirit as He asks us, "What are you expecting?" We must move past disappointments and fears regarding past seasons of barrenness or spiritual stillbirths and stir up a revival of our expectations before God in order to see our faith produce the breakthrough we have been carrying.

As a woman completes her ninth month her discomfort increases until the delivery. Sometimes she even feels miserable with emotions, sleepless nights, and pressure, but there is a joy set before her. That joy will give you grace to endure the times of challenge, knowing that when it becomes time to push your life will change forever!

But in Isaiah 37:3 Hezekiah declares "*for the children have come to birth, but there is no strength to bring them forth*" (NKJV). This prophecy was given to King Hezekiah, a righteous king who was a reformer, turning Judah back to God and restoring temple worship. He was faithful to the Lord, yet his city (Jerusalem) had become besieged by the cruel king of Assyria, Sennacherib, and was faced with certain destruction if God didn't intervene.

## The Rabshakeh Assignment

I had a dream where a spiritual assignment was sent against a godly leader. The enemy's name was Rabshakeh and he was coming to spread poison on the back of the leader and then take a rod and beat the back, driving the poison in and breaking the leader. (The back represents the place of a man's strength. Isaiah 22 talks about the burden in the valley of the vision.

The back was where Jesus was beaten so that we can receive our healing. But the enemy wanted to beat him down, afflict him with poison, rob healing, and destroy him.) But before Rabshakeh could complete his mission of destruction, we alerted the authorities who captured him. They then led us out and put rods in our hands to beat his back!

What does this dream have to do with the story of the besiegement of Jerusalem? It turns out that Rabshakeh was not the name of a reggae band but rather was the emissary of Sennacherib, his mouthpiece sent to demoralize Hezekiah and his armies, trying to get them to give up, lay down their weapons, and surrender the city. He tried to convince Hezekiah and his leaders that God had forsaken them and would not save them.

His name means "chief prince" and may well be a demonic assignment against true reformers and leaders today. Rabshakeh filled the air with accusations against who God is, against who the leaders are, and about the impossibility of their situation. Understand he was seeking to spread poison and get in their heads so that they would be beaten down and submit to giving up and being overthrown. Don't let the enemy get in your head! He will convince you that all your works of righteousness and reformation have been for nothing and that in the end God will abandon you and not hear your prayers. Is it possible to be pregnant with reformation and not bring it forth? Is it possible to be pregnant with your miracle answer and it be aborted or stillborn because you give up?

But rather than let Rabshakeh and his poisonous words rob them of their land, Hezekiah set himself to seek the Lord and to pray. He encouraged his people with these faith-filled words in the midst of desperate times:

> *Be strong and courageous, be not afraid nor dismayed for the*
> *king of Assyria, nor for all the multitude that is with him: for*
> *there be more with us than with him: with him is an arm of*
> *flesh; but with us is the Lord our God to help us, and to fight*

*our battles. And the people rested themselves upon the words
of Hezekiah king of Judah* (2 Chronicles 32:7-8 KJV).

He also sent for Isaiah the prophet to get a word from God for them. Isaiah came and told Hezekiah the Lord had heard his prayers. He would defend the city! He then released a prophetic word of breakthrough that sounded impossible. That night God sent an angel down who wiped out 185,000 Assyrians, and Rabshakeh and Sennacherib both returned to their own country only to be killed by their own. God fought for Judah! Prayer and prophecy shifted the battle and brought heavenly intervention! The prophet's reward was manifested as God mobilized the angel armies to overthrow the enemy. It was about this situation that Isaiah prophesied:

> *"No weapon formed against you shall prosper, and every tongue
> which rises against you in judgment you shall condemn. This is
> the heritage of the servants of the Lord, and their righteousness
> is from Me," says the Lord* (Isaiah 54:17 NKJV).

If you recall at the end of my dream the rod of punishment was used on the back of the enemy. Isaiah also prophesied about this, which is part of God's battle strategy for us today to break out of the survival of besiegement into revival for a new day.

> *The voice of the Lord will shatter Assyria [your enemy];
> with his rod he will strike them down. Every stroke the Lord
> lays on them with his punishing club will be to the music of
> timbrels and harps, as he fights them in battle with the blows
> of his arm* (Isaiah 30:31-32 NIV).

## THE VOICE OF THE LORD AND OUR PRAISE IS A WEAPON!

If you are in survival mode—*repent, pray, and prophesy!* If you feel besieged—repent, pray, and prophesy! If you need a miracle that looks impossible—repent, pray, and prophesy! If you are carrying reformation and revival—release the voice of God and it will shatter your enemy so you can bring it to birth! God will fight for you!

## THE NINTH HOUR OF PRAYER

In Scripture the ninth hour of the Jewish day was 3:00 in the afternoon (considered the ninth hour since daybreak). It was the time of prayer and evening sacrifice and was evidenced as a time when earthly prayers resulted in a heavenly response. *This year God is bringing the Church out of survival prayers into revival prayers.* There is a growing excitement about what God is doing in the earth that will cause our prayers to be less self-focused (survival focused) and more kingdom-focused. We will recognize that *prayer is the midwife that births miracles!* We will have such miracles breaking out to meet the personal needs that we can press in to focus on praying God's reformation purposes to be evidenced in culture and national transformation.

In First Kings 18:36-39 Elijah was on Mount Carmel in a showdown with the false prophets of Baal. While they were carrying on cutting themselves and chanting empty petitions to their false gods, Elijah prepared an altar with a sacrifice on it. It was a time of drought, yet Elijah poured precious water over his sacrifice, indicating his complete dependence on heaven to answer his prayers. In the ninth hour, at the time of evening sacrifice, God answered from heaven and sent fire to consume the sacrifice and lick up the water. The people were astounded by this supernatural display and immediately fell on their faces and turned their hearts back to God. This sign from heaven in the ninth hour released Elijah to slay the false prophets and broke the curse of drought off the land. They went from the survival of drought to a revival of faith toward God, which activated the prophetic release from Elijah, declaring, "I hear the sound of abundance of rain!" (see 1 Kings 18:41 NKJV). In this season, as God's people pray, God will send a response of Holy Spirit fire that will expose and oppose the "false prophets" of today—false religions and philosophies,

139

false prognosticators in media, and false reformation movements in culture that misconstrue justice. It's time to see spiritual drought broken and revival break out!

In Ezra 9 and 10 we see Ezra prayed national revival prayers for the Jews at the time of the evening sacrifice (the ninth hour). As a result of his intercession the nation returned to the God of their fathers and repented of their sin of marrying pagan wives, losing their distinctiveness as a holy people. God heard their prayers, their repentance, and restored them to His heart. More and more the Church will be Kingdom influencers within culture but with a distinctiveness of holiness that also sets them apart as a counter culture. It's only as we are salt and light that we can drive out darkness.

In Daniel 9 Daniel too prayed revival prayers interceding for his nation, repenting on behalf of their sin and separation from God, realizing that it was time for their 70 years of captivity in Babylon to come to an end. It was time for repentance, restoration, and reformation in the land. At the ninth hour, the angel Gabriel appeared and began to give Daniel understanding and instruction. We are coming into a time of angelic encounters in which we are not just comforted or inspired by the presence of angels, but rather are empowered with clarity and insight for the days ahead. The angel's instruction enabled Daniel to lead God's people in a national shift out of the survival of captivity into a revival as God's people with a vision to repossess their promised inheritance.

In the New Testament we see several powerful displays of heaven being moved by the prayers of men in the ninth hour. In Acts 3:1 Peter and John were at the Gate Beautiful (meaning the appointed place at a favorable, appointed time) at the ninth hour of prayer when they encountered a lame man begging alms. He was living in a state of survival—begging just to survive. He lived with no victory, no breakthrough, no ability to move forward, no joy, no vision for his future that was different from the daily grind. But rather than giving him earthly riches to meet a temporal need, which would have left him in a survival state, Peter and John met his need that money couldn't buy and released healing to him. His survival status as a lame man was immediately shifted to a man who carried revival as he leapt to his feet and praised God, demonstrating God's reality to all who knew him. His vision for life was revived! His joy was revived! His faith in God was revived! I believe this is a picture of not just miracles for individuals, but a picture of God's revival, rejuvenating, restoring power over every area in which the Church has been lame, dysfunctional, or limited in hope or vision for the future. God's power will cause an inactive, incapacitated, weak, and limited Church to burst out with a renewed hope and confidence that activates "divine reversals" in every circumstance.

In Acts 10 we see the story of the Roman centurion, Cornelius, who is crying out to the Lord for salvation. He was a devout man who feared God and gave generously to the poor. Again, in the ninth hour (the Jewish hour of prayer even though he was a Gentile), an angel visits him and says that his prayers and his giving have opened a door in the spirit realm that got God's attention. The angel then instructs him to send for Peter who will explain the path to salvation. The result is the gospel of the Kingdom is first preached to a Gentile and his whole household is saved, filled with the Holy Spirit, and baptized in water. There was a supernatural grace to not just save Cornelius but his entire household. We need to renew our prayers for prodigals and pre-believing family members to come to Christ; however, we must also understand that this whole story speaks of a new era beginning of nations turning to the Lord. This encounter opened up the Gentile world to the gospel. Be prepared for the Lord to begin to visit unbelievers in dreams, visions, and even angelic encounters, which will break down the walls that have thus far kept them out of the Kingdom. Get ready for harvest! Prepare for revival!

One of the most powerful ninth hour stories, when the intercession of men caused heaven to connect with earth, is the day Jesus Christ was crucified. He was hung on the cross in the third hour (about 9:00 a.m.), but at the ninth hour He cried out, "My God, my God, why have you forsaken Me?" He then declared, "It is finished," and died. The declaration "It is finished" is exactly what the priest would declare at the time of evening sacrifice after shedding the blood of the sacrificial lamb for the sins of the people. Jesus became our intercessor and the perfect sacrifice for the sin of all humanity. It was in that same hour that the veil of the temple was torn from top to bottom, the ground shook, and the dead were resurrected and appeared in the cities. All this in the ninth hour! God is declaring that the veil of separation (shame, fear, inadequacy, powerlessness, etc.) that many have felt kept them out of His holy presence is coming down, the heavens are being ripped open, and a fresh access is being given to the goodness, power, revelation, and wisdom from His throne room of grace. Everything that can be shaken will be shaken. But the shaking will result in revival, resurrection life, an awakening of dry bones that will cause the world to declare, "Truly, Jesus is the Son of God!"

It is the ninth hour! Let's shift from survival mode to a revival mode! Let's raise our expectations and increase our prayer focus to birth the vision God has given. Let's get Rabshakeh's lies out of our heads. Let's release the voice of the Lord to shatter the enemy. Let's push in prayer and the power of the Holy Spirit to see a nation born in a day. Let's receive our prophet's reward. God will fight for us!

# About Jane Hamon

JANE HAMON SERVES, WITH HER HUSBAND TOM, AS SENIOR PASTOR of Vision Church @ Christian International. In their nearly 30 years of ministry together, they have built a thriving local church, traveled to more than 50 nations, and helped to lead Christian International Ministries, founded by Dr. Bill Hamon. A clear prophetic voice and eloquent teacher, Jane Hamon travels extensively ministering at national and international conferences, consulting with leaders, and teaching at Bible colleges. She is frequently featured on a variety of Christian television programs. A gifted storyteller, she has sprinkled her three books—*Dreams and Visions, The Deborah Company,* and *The Cyrus Decree*—with rich personal experiences, extensive research, and valuable teaching. Jane attended Christ for the Nations Institute in Dallas, Texas, and later received a Bachelor of Theology and an honorary Doctorate of Divinity from Christian International School of Theology. Jane makes her home in beautiful Santa Rosa Beach, Florida, where she enjoys fulfilling some of her favorite roles in life as wife, mother, and now "Mimi" to her growing number of grandchildren.

# THE LORD IS AN AVENGER

*Michael L. Brown*

THERE IS A POPULAR TEACHING IN THE CHARISMATIC CHURCH these days that claims that God is not pouring out judgment in the present age because Jesus took all our judgment at the cross. Not only is this unscriptural, it is unhelpful. I believe in the days ahead there will be a course correction, and many who have embraced this teaching will renounce it.

I understand, of course, why some are teaching this. They believe it enhances our understanding of the goodness of God, removes a distorted picture of the Lord from the eyes of the world (as if He's always angry and vengeful), and glorifies the work of Jesus on the cross. So, the motivation for this doctrine may be good, and there are certainly positive aspects to it, especially when we realize how many believers live in fear and condemnation. And I agree that it is crucial that these precious saints come to know the Father's love so they feel safe and secure in His arms. But the pendulum has swung way too far, and this new teaching is fundamentally wrong and must be rejected.

Before we look at some key Scriptures, let me ask a simple question: If it's true that the Lord is not pouring out judgment and wrath in the present age, because Jesus took all judgment on Himself on the cross, why, then, will He pour His wrath in the future? You might say, "But today is the age of grace. At the end of this age, the world will no longer be under grace and that's when God's judgment will be poured out."

But that begs the question, because the issue is not whether we're in the age of grace or not. The issue is this: If Jesus took all judgment at the cross, why will there *ever* be judgment in the future? I have yet to receive a biblically coherent answer to this question.

And make no mistake about it—*the wrath of God is coming*. Just look at these references to God's wrath in the New Testament:

> *Whoever believes in the Son has eternal life; whoever does not obey the Son shall not see life, but the wrath of God remains on him* (John 3:36 ESV).

> *For the wrath of God is revealed from heaven against all ungodliness and unrighteousness of men, who by their unrighteousness suppress the truth* (Romans 1:18 ESV).

> *Since, therefore, we have now been justified by his blood, much more shall we be saved by him from the wrath of God* (Romans 5:9 ESV).

> *Beloved, never avenge yourselves, but leave it to the wrath of God, for it is written, "Vengeance is mine, I will repay, says the Lord"* (Romans 12:19 ESV).

*Let no one deceive you with empty words, for because of these things the wrath of God comes upon the sons of disobedience* (Ephesians 5:6 ESV).

*On account of these the wrath of God is coming* (Colossians 3:6 ESV).

*So the angel swung his sickle across the earth and gathered the grape harvest of the earth and threw it into the great winepress of the wrath of God* (Revelation 14:19 ESV).

*Then I saw another sign in heaven, great and amazing, seven angels with seven plagues, which are the last, for with them the wrath of God is finished* (Revelation 15:1 ESV).

*And one of the four living creatures gave to the seven angels seven golden bowls full of the wrath of God who lives forever and ever* (Revelation 15:7 ESV).

*Then I heard a loud voice from the temple telling the seven angels, "Go and pour out on the earth the seven bowls of the wrath of God"* (Revelation 16:1 ESV).

*From his mouth comes a sharp sword with which to strike down the nations, and he will rule them with a rod of iron. He will tread the winepress of the fury of the wrath of God the Almighty* (Revelation 19:15 ESV).

I ask again: If there is no wrath and judgment for the present age because Jesus took it all on the cross, why will there be wrath and judgment at the end of this age? Why will Jesus return *"in flaming fire, inflicting vengeance on those who do not know God and on those who do not obey the gospel of our Lord Jesus"* (2 Thess. 1:8 ESV)? And when He returns, why will those who oppose Him *"suffer the punishment of eternal destruction, away from the presence of the Lord and from the glory of his might*" (2 Thess. 1:9 ESV)? And why does Revelation speak so much the outpouring of God's wrath?

Some would say, "But the Book of Revelation was written for the early Church. We should interpret it in a preterist (past) way."

But that too begs the question, because that would mean the wrath of God was poured out on sinners in the first or second centuries—again, *after* Jesus died for our sins on the cross. Why was there judgment then but not now? Wasn't the New Testament Church living in the age of grace?

Yes, it is gloriously true that Jesus *fully* paid for our sins. There's nothing we can add to it, no act of penance we can do to deserve it, no service or prayer or deed we can offer to supplement the cross. When He said, "It is finished," He meant every word of it. He did everything He needed to do to fulfill prophecy and to complete His work of dying in our place, then rising from the dead for our vindication.

But it is also true that those who reject His grace will receive His judgment. That's why Paul urged the believers in Rome to note carefully "*the kindness and the severity of God: severity toward those who have fallen [speaking of the Jews who rejected the Messiah], but God's kindness to you [speaking to Gentile believers], provided you continue in his kindness. Otherwise you too will be cut off*" (Rom. 11:22 ESV). That sounds like a warning to me—and not just for the distant future. These words are relevant today.

Those who claim God does not judge today have to do all kinds of exegetical summersaults to explain away His judgment on Ananias and Sapphira in Acts 5 (as a result of which "*great fear came upon the whole church and upon all who heard of these things*"—Acts 5:11 ESV) and His judgment on Herod (see Acts 12:20-24). They also have to change Paul's words in First Corinthians 11, as if he was speaking about unbelievers when he wrote that some of them had fallen asleep and others were sick because they partook of the Lord's table unworthily (see 1 Cor. 11:27-32).

The fact is that Paul only used "fall asleep" for the death of believers, and his words at the end of this chapter are unmistakably clear: *"But if we judged ourselves truly, we would not be judged. But when we are judged by the Lord, we are disciplined so that we may not be condemned along with the world"* (1 Cor. 11:31-32 ESV).

And what about the words of Jesus, spoken to the church of Thyatira, in Revelation? How do these line up with the doctrine of "no divine judgment in the present age"? The Lord said:

> *I have this against you, that you tolerate that woman Jezebel, who calls herself a prophetess and is teaching and seducing my servants to practice sexual immorality and to eat food sacrificed to idols. I gave her time to repent, but she refuses to repent of her sexual immorality. Behold, I will throw her onto a sickbed, and those who commit adultery with her I will throw into great tribulation, unless they repent of her works, and I will strike her children dead. And all the churches will know that I am he who searches mind and heart, and I will give to each of you according to your works* (Revelation 2:20-23).

Those are the words of our compassionate Savior. Those are the words of the Lord of all grace. But He is also the Lord of judgment—in this age and in the age to come. To deny this to deny fundamental aspects of His nature.

The psalmist understood this, calling on the whole world to rejoice *because God was coming to judge the wicked* (see Ps. 96, 98). If they refuse to repent, that's a good thing, not a bad thing. And while the Lord desires that all will come to repentance (see 1 Tim. 2:1-4; 2 Pet. 3:9), He will rightly mete out judgment on those who refuse to repent. His righteousness and justice require it.

Judgment on the ungodly means salvation for the godly, and that's a reason to rejoice. In fact, if the Lord didn't bring judgment on the wicked—in this world and/or in the world to come—then He would not be a good God.

Paul understood this well, reminding his readers about the Lord's vengeance. When it came to sexual purity and adultery, he urged:

> That no one transgress and wrong his brother in this matter, because **the Lord is an avenger** in all these things, as we told you beforehand and solemnly warned you. For God has not called us for impurity, but in holiness. Therefore whoever disregards this, disregards not man but God, who gives his Holy Spirit to you (1 Thessalonians 4:6-8 ESV).

And note carefully the context: He was warning believers not to play games with God's holiness.

And why does Paul exhort us not to take matters into our hands and pay back evil for evil? Because the Lord is the one who will do this: "*Beloved, never avenge yourselves, but leave it to the wrath of God, for it is written, 'Vengeance is mine, I will repay, says the Lord'*" (Rom. 12:19). Yes, leave it to the Avenger!

As for believers who think that they can sin willfully and deliberately and yet find some kind of atonement outside the cross (this was a special temptation to the early Jewish believers), the writer of Hebrews wrote this:

> For if we go on sinning deliberately after receiving the knowledge of the truth, there no longer remains a sacrifice for sins, but a fearful expectation of judgment, and a fury of fire that will consume the adversaries. Anyone who has set aside the law of Moses dies without mercy on the evidence of two or three witnesses. How much worse punishment, do you think, will be deserved by the one who has trampled underfoot the

*Son of God, and has profaned the blood of the covenant by which he was sanctified, and has outraged the Spirit of grace? For we know him who said, "Vengeance is mine; I will repay." And again, "The Lord will judge his people." It is a fearful thing to fall into the hands of the living God"* (Hebrews 10:26-31).

At the risk of being redundant, let me state again that this was written to *warn believers,* and within just a few short verses the author spoke of divine judgment and wrath more than many preachers do in a year (or a lifetime). And this is the Word of God, not the opinion of people. This is sacred truth—glorious, liberating truth.

And while it's true that I have not quoted a single verse here from the Old Testament (other than referencing the Psalms), both Paul and the author of Hebrews freely quoted from it. All of this is God's Word, and all of it is relevant for us today.

Even for those who wrongly believe that God does not pour out judgment in the present age, there's no excuse for not preaching about the wrath to come, a common theme in the New Testament. Or, to put this in the form of a question—if Paul thought it was important to warn about the coming wrath, why don't we feel it's important? (Note that I've hardly said anything about the future punishment of hell, just the wrath to come on the earth.)

I personally affirm the glorious message of grace and the emphasis on the goodness of God. But part of God's goodness is His justice, and that means He is a righteous Judge. And those who refuse the God of grace will encounter the God of judgment.

Understanding this helps us to recover the fear of the Lord, a glorious theme in both the Old and New Testaments (see Prov. 1:7; Acts 9:31). I believe that is a theme and a truth that will be recovered in the days ahead.

# About Michael Brown

Dr. Michael L. Brown holds a Ph.D. in Near Eastern Languages and Literatures from New York University and has served as a visiting or adjunct professor at seven top seminaries. The author of more than 30 books, he hosts the *Line of Fire* radio program, a syndicated, daily talk show, where he serves as "your voice of moral, cultural, and spiritual revolution," and his syndicated columns appear on many Christian and conservative websites. He also hosts TV programs airing on NRBTV, GOD TV, and METV, and he has appeared as a guest on secular and Christian media (including Piers Morgan, Tyra Banks, Phil Donahue, *700 Club*, and Daystar). He has conducted debates or outreach lectures on major campuses, including Oxford University, the Hebrew University (Jerusalem), Ohio State University, Yale, and USC. Michael and his wife, Nancy, have two children and four grandchildren. They live near Charlotte, NC.

# ENTERING THE NEW ERA

*Tim Sheets*

GOD DEALS WITH ME THROUGH VISIONS—IT'S BEEN THIS WAY since I was a small child. It is one of the main ways He speaks to me. Recently, I received a vision of a funnel, and the top part of the funnel resembled a television screen. On that screen there were scenes scrolling across, beginning with Acts 2 events and continuing until present day. Just scene after scene of Church history, like a video highlight of outpourings and revival movements. All of these scenes were flowing down from the funnel, from the widest portion at the top (the bowl) and being squeezed into the narrow pipe at the bottom of the funnel—running directly into our present times. It was like watching a movie.

Not wanting to surmise regarding this vision, I said, "Holy Spirit, what are You showing me?" Holy Spirit replied, "I'm pouring the anointings

153

and streams of the ages into the New Era we've prepared for the glorious ekklesia." I then said, "What am I to do with this?" He said, "Declare it is connected to its moment, it has intersected with its moment—the convergence has begun."

He continued to speak to me about the convergence of the ages. He said:

> "Pray it. Decree it. Prophesy it. Guard it with governing intercession. Study it. And then, steward its activation into the world with Me. The angels of alignment have aligned the convergence. And now begins the flow of purpose—purposes and proposed purpose that have been prophesied into your times."

Holy Spirit continued, "Activate the ekklesia to flow with the new flow! It will accelerate rapidly to fullness." At this point it became more like a prophecy:

> "For you have entered a fullness of times. You are entering the second apostolic age. It will be an era of signs—wonders—miracles—healings. It will be the era when the ekklesia sits on the throne of regions and, yes, even nations, influencing through our spiritual Kingdom, influencing through spirit-governing language and intercession for the natural kingdom in the earth realm.
>
> "Watch the ekklesia rise! It is purposed. It shall be so! It will rise and rule as intended; it has now connected to its moment. Watch the change and changes. Declare the change and changes. Align with heaven and you will see it on earth. Align with heaven and activate the rapid change. Speak your agreement. Speak to the fog. Command it to lift. Then you will see the new era. It will be manifestly revealed."

After all of this He quickened again to me the following prophetic word:

"Holy Spirit says to the remnant warriors, it is time for the unveiling. The great season has now come and the curtain is being drawn and the world will now see the scintillating Kingdom of King Jesus rising from the ashes of a beguiled world. See it, says the Lord. See its radiant glory. It is intensifying, accelerating, and revealing your King as the supreme commander of heaven and of earth. It's time for the reveal of the supernatural into the natural, says the Lord. There will now be seen a spiritual Kingdom that visibly affects the world. It will visibly affect the marketplace, the education system, and the media. Like leaven, the mighty Kingdom of God and His Christ will penetrate the earth as never before. No more delay, says heaven. Darkness will now be penetrated and dispelled by glorious light. Deception will be dispelled by glorious truth. Iniquity will be uprooted by glorious power. Demon thrones will be toppled by glorious authority, dominating authority, supreme authority, and ruling and reigning authority. Bondage will be broken by glorious liberty. Curses will now be reversed by glorious blessings. Principalities and powers, mights and dominions will be toppled by the superior forces of My Kingdom, says the Lord of Hosts. My Kingdom is rising and it will now be revealed in new ways and in new displays. It cannot be stopped. It cannot be hindered. It cannot be compromised. My spiritual Kingdom will visibly affect this world. It will rise. It will rule, and it will reign with wisdom and with awesome power. It has been, it is, and it will be increasing upon the earth with jealous aggression and with striking power from heaven flashing down to your planet, says the Lord.

Yes, a Kingdom that has no end and no equal will now be revealed as promised.

"The surge of heaven has now begun. The world has never seen the like—a functioning spiritual Kingdom that's at hand. You can touch it. It is among you, a Kingdom that is coming. It keeps coming and coming and coming, and is coming until an even greater reveal—My coming in the clouds of glory. For you are entering into the season of the mighty King who prevails, a King who will make His stand. His Kingdom is growing and His Kingdom will prevail. And the prevailing anointing of Jesus will now be seen upon His remnant people. As in His first ekklesia, so mightily grew the Word and it prevailed—so it will be in your times. Anointing to prevail is now being poured out among you. You will prevail. The King's Word on your lips will prevail mightily. Speak on the King's behalf. Speak His Word from your lips. Speak as ambassadors in His Kingdom, and as you speak you will grow. Promises believed for will grow and they will prevail to fullness before your eyes. Prophetic words will prevail to fullness. My Word will not return void. Supernatural deliverance will now prevail to fullness. Healings and miracles will now prevail to fullness. Dreams and visions will now prevail to fullness. It is "yes" and it is "amen" in heaven. My Church will prevail, says the Lord. The gates of hell will not prevail. The authority of hell cannot prevail. It is written and it cannot be reversed. It is the immutable decree of your King, so act in accordant confidence. Yes, says the Lord, the convergence of the ages has begun and My Kingdom will expand mightily."

God has spoken to me and shown me so clearly what we are stepping into and what He is about to do in us and through us. There is an urgency, an expectancy, and unprecedented acceleration as we recognize that we are intersecting with His plan and purpose. This is the season we have been prepared for.

# About Tim Sheets

Tim Sheets is an apostle, pastor of The Oasis Church in Middletown, Ohio, the founder of Awakening Now Prayer Network, and author. He travels extensively throughout the United States, Canada, and other nations, carrying his heart and vision for awakening and reformation. He teaches and ministers in conferences, Bible colleges, seminars and churches, releasing the authority of the believer and an anointing for signs, wonders, and miracles.

# THE TRUST OF GOD, WEALTH TRANSFER, AND A MERGING OF MANTLES

*Fiorella Giordano*

T HE YEAR 2019 IS APPOINTED TO BE A YEAR OF THE *FEAR OF THE Lord* that will restore the wonder and awe of God to the Church and the world. It will birth forth healing, wealth, salvation. A new breed of vessels carries exponential creative authority, and a new breed of messengers are marked by the fire of God, carrying a threefold cord in their mantles of intimacy, power, and healing.

## THE TRUST OF GOD

I heard the Lord speak to me about His trust fund for 2019—the fund and realm of resources that are given to those who are walking in maturity and purity. Just like in the natural, trust funds are given to the recipients when they come of age; so it is in the spirit. He is positioning His mature sons and daughters into places of influence and effectiveness. I believe that this year we are going to begin to see many vessels, regions, and cities enter into the *trust of the Lord*, in a wealth of salvation, wisdom, knowledge, and stability of time, because they have esteemed and held the Lord above all else.

> *How great is your goodness, which You have stored up for those who fear You, which You have wrought for those who take refuge in You, before the sons of men!* (Psalm 31:19)

> *The Lord is exalted, for He dwells on high; He has filled Zion with justice and righteousness. And He will be the stability of your times, a wealth of salvation, wisdom and knowledge; the fear of God is his treasure* (Isaiah 33:5-6).

## UNLOCKING THE REALMS OF HEALING FOR A HEALING AWAKENING

As the spirit of the fear of the Lord is released this year, we are going to begin to not only see a restoration of holiness and awe but also a tangible increase of the realms of healing and miracles. It will lead the way to a healing movement, with a marked emphasis on creative miracles—not only in physiological dimensions but also miracles of the heart, soul, and mind.

> *Do not be wise in your own eyes; fear the Lord and turn away from evil. It will be healing to your body and refreshment to your bones* (Proverbs 3:7-8).

## TRANSFER OF WEALTH AND ECONOMY SOLUTIONS

The realm of wealth is deeply connected to the fear of the Lord, and this year will be key in unlocking new resources and untapped sources of wealth. God is going to give vision and wisdom to those who have been found faithful. He will bring an unveiling of discoveries in the realms of finance and resources. Things that human eyes had not been able to see before will be unveiled, mechanisms of economy systems and time will be unlocked, for there is a redemption that has been ordained for this year. Insights into the dimension of time and its facets of redemption will accompany this realm.

The economy of the redeemed timetable of God will be laid out and blueprints into understanding these times will come forth, bringing insight into the divine patterns of the redemption God has ordained that exceedingly surpasses the curses of toil and poverty. These insights will begin to unlock the minds of people and the constraints of times past will be removed—impossibilities will be removed. There is a change of understanding that many will undergo this year, and it will bring them into an ample land full of potential and opportunity and fruitfulness.

> *The reward of humility and the fear of the Lord are riches, honor and life* (Proverbs 22:4).

> *Therefore be careful how you walk, not as unwise men but as wise, making the most of your time, because the day are evil* (Ephesians 5:15-16).

## THE SECRET OF THE LORD

This year God is going to begin to unveil deeper realms of His glory and mysteries to His friends—the deep things of God. Those who have hungered and thirsted after Him will be given incredible access into fresh insight, wisdom, and understanding. This will bring forth the increase of the knowledge of God in the earth. It will stir many to seek God, and to pursue His heart and purposes. This key of intimacy will unlock realms of worship and praise that the earth has not experienced before. The glory of God is going to visit the realm of sound. His glory will move through the testimony of His children. He will move as they fill the atmosphere with the sound of the eternal life they have experienced in the secret place. This will touch the spheres of the arts and media. Deep intimacy will birth a new expression of devotion and worship in the sound of His people. It will stir a greater depth of prayer, and it will unleash a fresh grace for harvest and missions.

> *The secret of the Lord is for those who fear Him, and He will make them know His covenant* (Psalm 25:14).

## A New Breed: The Merging of Three Mantles—Elijah, Enoch, and John G. Lake

In the dream I found myself surrounded by the cloud of witnesses. I was escorted into a deep crevice in the cleft of the rock, and I was told that it was the cave where Elijah and Enoch had accessed the deep places that they had touched in God. The cave was a symbol of depth and the secret of the Lord. I could feel the realms of God these two prophets had walked in.

As I walked through this place I could feel a flame within my heart; it grew more vehement as I was there. It was like the testimony of these two prophets was in the very atmosphere. My heart was marked like the heart of the ones who walked with Jesus on the road to Emmaus, because I could feel the uncompromising flame of Christ in the midst of this place.

> *They said to one another, "Were not our hearts burning within us while He was speaking to us on the road, while He was explaining the Scriptures to us?"* (Luke 24:32)

This fire within my heart was so fierce that all I could feel was the commissioning of God over my being, full of purpose, unveiling what He had written for my life. All I could hear and feel was the calling of God calling me to be a messenger, a voice. As I became baptized in this fire, I became completely consumed with the truth of my calling and the truth of divine design. I understood at this moment that I had been brought to this place to be shown the type of messengers who are being sent from before the throne of God and the unveiling that will come upon their hearts as they enter the deep places God is calling them into.

The bright and burning ones have a flame in their hearts that is powerful and will burn and consume anything and everything that is not part of their call, extinguishing even the sound of voices that are not in unison with the One who called them.

As this was happening, I saw a man come into the realm where I was. It was John G. Lake, and I had a very strong impression that his mantle and anointing would be merged with that of Elijah and Enoch for this hour. What he carried in the realms of healing and science was going to be activated over a breed of prophets. As I saw him enter in, he began to speak to me about the threefold realm of sanctification and the realms and paths of life according to Psalm 16:11:

> *You will make known to me the path of life; in Your presence*
> *is fullness of joy; in Your right hand there are pleasure forever.*

He called this the embrace of the 777. I understood the parable in the numbers—it spoke of a triune fullness. These numbers stood as keys of the fullness of the first commandment—you shall love your God with all your heart, soul, and mind (see Matt. 22:37). I also understood that the embrace that he spoke of was abiding in the presence of God, who is the very source of all life, according to John 15:4: *"Abide in Me, and I in you. As the branch cannot bear fruit of itself unless it abides in the vine, so neither can you unless you abide in Me."*

Embracing Him in every dimension of our being is what will begin to birth forth the realm of healing beyond gifts and graces of healing. Here I saw many pools or reservoirs of healing. Each one was like a realm, carrying an atmospheric influence and air of supremacy, like Peter's shadow that could heal the sick. These realms of healing weren't only for healing the physically sick; there were also realms carrying thought leadership in the realms of life that God wants to release on the earth—new trends of thought that carry healing and solutions. In addition to this, I also sensed that God was preparing and commissioning messengers who would be ministers of these realms and that the earth was about to be visited not just with a tsunami wave of healing but everlasting life flowing through burning, pure vessels who had been marked with divine fire.

As this download saturated my spirit, a man from the cloud of witnesses began to prophesy about the harmonics of this threefold mantle. He prayed and prophesied that the harmony in the anointing would create a new sound that would brood over the ones carrying these mantles—a sound to create, a sound to do a multiverse of things. Its amplitude was wide, allowing for these vessels to move in and out of many arenas not constrained by times and ruled by eternity. These vessels will carry authority to touch every mountain of society.

## NEW HYBRID OF PROPHETS

These men and women will carry great power, great insight into mystical realms, and incredible fruit of life and healing. It will be marked by sound doctrine, rooted in the Word of God.

They are mantled to be restorers of the desolations of many generations, marked with intimate friendship with God, entrusted with deep realms of glory, marked with supernatural abilities beyond the confines of space and time. They are marked with tremendous power followed by remarkable signs and wonders in the heavens and the earth, carrying healing beyond gifting and beyond anointings. Stadiums and healing ministries will be just the beginning for this new breed, for they are called to heal nations, to heal the earth. They will know deeply the encouragement of heaven, for there is a great cloud surrounding them in this hour.

They will be a fresh expression of the heart of God for this generation. These prophets will carry a threefold mantle of Elijah, Enoch, and John G. Lake. They are courageous, jealous for the name of God with a fire that cannot be quenched, with national and international assignments. They carry deep revelatory insight that will give a grid for the heavenly increase that is coming. Carrying a grace for manifestation, attesting to the hand of God in their lives, they will not only give vision but also bring into manifestation what God has appointed to manifest through them.

## The Sevenfold Unveiling of His Light

God's justice is being released in a powerful way over the ones who have been obscured by the enemy—those who have been overlooked and rejected. The Spirit of God has appointed 2019 as a year of great light and unveiling. There is a sevenfold justice of radiance and light appointed over many people. The manifestation of the light of God will be incredibly evident by the marked favor these will carry. They will be vessels who will carry the radiance of the glory of God and will carry great creative authority because of the realm of light they are being entrusted with. They are not only extinguishing darkness wherever they go but also bringing forth the new things from God—what no eye has seen or ear heard. They carry a sevenfold day of creative glory. Part of their assignment will be to bring visibility to the things God is saying and doing. They will bring vision wherever they go, and the light of His presence will be upon them, and what they put their hands to will shine with His light.

> *The light of the moon will be as the light of the sun, and the light of the sun will be seven times brighter, like the light of seven days, on the day the Lord binds up the fracture of His people and heals the bruise He has inflicted* (Isaiah 30:26).

# About Fiorella Giordano

Fiorella Giordano is a speaker, worship leader, poet, and creative, who functions as Seer, discerning the destiny of different spheres of society, especially Media, Music, Art, Technology, Science, and Government. She carries deep insight into times and seasons and their dispensations, over this generation, movements, and spheres, and nations. She had a season of angelic visitations in 2011 that marked her life, with deep understanding concerning sound, the realms of eternity, creation, and abundant life. Her deepest desire is to see this earth transformed by the manifestation of the resurrection and life of Jesus, expressed in its renewed nature as a new creation. She currently resides in the Dallas area, and is part of Freedom International Church in Waxahachie, Texas.

# What Time Is It? A Glance into 2019 and Beyond

*James W. Goll*

As time goes marching by, we find an escalation of activity in the Spirit world being mirrored in the natural realm. Both dimensions are a reflection of the intensity of the battle in the heavenlies as the last-days battles kick into higher gear. These are critical times and these are days of great advances as well.

I have not personally known a season like this when the activity in the spirit world is this heightened in possibly 30 years. Having close to 45 years of full-time vocational ministry under my belt, it allows me to speak from a veteran perspective. With that in mind, let me give you a few bullet points as a partial attempt to describe the days in which we live and are crossing a threshold into.

## Five Clear Words for 2019 and Beyond

The first point I want to emphasize is that *God has the harvest on His mind*. These are the days of the rebirthing of the evangelist. As Billy Graham graduated into heaven, a mantle for the evangelist has fallen. This mantle is not one that has descended on just one man or one woman, but rather a calling of grace from God granted to an entire generation. There is an influx of souls coming into the Kingdom unlike anything we have seen in the Body of Christ for 50 years.

It is time for the words of the prophet-seer Bob Jones—for the one billion soul harvest, especially among the youth, to come in. It is time for P.E. classes in God's school of the Holy Spirit. Yes, it is time for *prophetic evangelism* done outside the four walls of the church. Power encounters in the streets, miracles in the marketplace, prophetic revelation released in a relational context will become daily experiences. Why? *God has the harvest on His mind!*

Second, there is the deepening polarization taking place in society that will not be healed quickly. In fact, things are going to heat up. I was warned on this last Day of Atonement that there would be an increase of gang violence and a national problem where a huge arsenal of munitions would be distributed within the nation(s) by a devilish sinister plot to create disorder and chaos and senseless crimes. I saw multiple mass shootings taking place in different cities around the world, like what occurred in Las Vegas, Nevada.

I was also shown gun raids where federal agents in the U.S. would confiscate massive arsenals. The Holy Spirit called this deepening polarization *the time of the great divide*. Now this prophetic point requires the response of intercession and spiritual warfare to expose the spirit of violence resulting in riots, division, and polarization. The words of Second Chronicles 7:14 are just as true today as the day they were originally written:

> *If My people who are called by My name will humble them-*
> *selves, and pray and seek My face, and turn from their wicked*
> *ways, then I will hear from heaven, and will forgive their sin*
> *and heal their land* (NKJV).

God is never taken by surprise. He is not in heaven with sweaty palms and God is not wringing His hands in a nervous frenzy. In fact, according to Job 36:32, *"He covers His hands with lightning [glory] and commands it to strike the mark."* Darkness is but an excellent backdrop for the times when the light shines the brightest. If history books are written in the future about the days we are entering into, they could be called *the days of His presence.* These are the days of great displays of His brilliant presence. Some have referred to these days as *the greatest show on earth.*

Watch as the emphasis increases on the theme of His presence in con-ferences, and teaching series spread throughout the global Body of Christ. There will be an outright invasion of the Holy Spirit taking over worship services and even large concert events with the awe and wonder of God as His manifest presence comes rolling in. After all, the distinguishing characteristic of the people of God is His presence among us (see Exod. 33:13-16).

A fourth clear point is that we have entered into days of acceleration and the "times of the suddenlies." I was given a dream encounter where I was climbing a hill and getting tired and weary. Finally, I made it to the top of the mountain at the time of the rising of the sun when the sky was electrified with a glorious display of His presence. The weariness of work-ing so hard dissipated, and I heard the voice of the Holy Spirit say, *"You have entered into the times of the suddenlies."*

Later that same day, when ministering at a NOW conference in my hometown of Nashville, Tennessee, I gained more understanding and the following phrases leapt into my comprehension: *"When the fullness of preparation meets the fullness of time it results in the time of the suddenlies."* It is like a woman giving birth to a child. There are long months of formation followed by uncomfortable times of stretching. Right when the expectant mother often feels she cannot carry this child any longer, that she can take no more, suddenly transition kicks into gear and the greatly desired birth appears. We are entering into the "times of the suddenlies."

Last, I want to drive home a point that many of us have been addressing for some years. In these days of the harvest when His presence increases and thesuddenlies of God appear on the scene, part of this fullness of preparation is due to the authentic *joining of the generations*. God desires to be manifested as the God of three generations in a generation. He longs that the wisdom of the older, combined with the resources of the middle, and then mixed with the necessary ingredient of the zeal of the younger generation all comes together. That is a recipe for a sustained move of God.

I am now not only a father in the natural but a grandfather of a growing number of grandchildren. I find myself beginning to fulfill a role in the Body of Christ that I honestly never saw myself doing. I knew I was called to be a father in my generation. But could it be that I have been saved from near-death experiences four different times because I am to be one of the grandfathers in our days and times? It appears that is the case. God is jealous for the authentic joining of the generations.

## WHEN THE GENERATIONS COME TOGETHER

Bishop Bill Hamon of Christian International has called these the "days of the saints." According to Ephesians 4:11, Christ who descended also ascended and gave gifts to men and women. Some are set apart to be pastors and teachers and others to be evangelists and yet others prophets and apostles. How long are these ministering office gifts of the Holy Spirit given? *"Until we all attain to the unity of the faith, and of the knowledge of the Son of God, to a mature man, to the measure of the stature which belongs to the fullness of Christ"* (Eph. 4:13). Well, this work of unity and maturity has not fully happened yet. Therefore, all five of these greatly needed ministry gifts are still being released. In fact, we have just entered into the second apostolic age of the Church.

This point was driven home to me recently when I went back to minister at Harvest Fellowship Church in Warrensburg, Missouri—the church where I was the co-founder around 40 years ago. I had my youngest daughter, Rachel Tucker, and her daughter, Ruby, with me on this trip. That was three generations in a generation in the same house of the Lord together. But not only that, my father, Wayne Goll, ran a lumberyard an hour and a half north on Highway 13. He helped us with the materials to build this very church building all those many years ago.

Though my dad had graduated to his heavenly reward over 20 years ago, I seemed aware that he was looking in upon the scene from the great cloud of witnesses. So it dawned on me while sitting on the front row during the presence-led worship that my father had his hand in this as well. That would be four generations having been involved. I was overcome with gratitude. The Holy Spirit seemed to like what was going on and whispered to me, *"This is the power of the joining of the generations."*

## WHAT TIME IS IT?

The Book of Romans contains more than only the great plan of salvation. It also carries the plan of how to live an effective Christian life in the midst of dark storms that may come. It is a book that teaches us what time it is and how to rule and reign with Christ Jesus in practical ways.

Romans 13:11-14 aptly portrays:

*Do this, knowing the time, that it is already the hour for you to awaken from sleep; for now salvation is nearer to us than when we believed. The night is almost gone, and the day is near. Therefore let us lay aside the deeds of darkness and put on the armor of light. Let us behave properly as in the day, not in carousing and drunkenness, not in sexual promiscuity and sensuality, not in strife and jealousy. But put on the Lord Jesus Christ, and make no provision for the flesh in regard to its lusts.*

## A Prayer of Consecration

*Gracious Father, we come to You in the mighty name of the Lord Jesus Christ. We thank You that we have been born for such as time as this and granted the honor to participate in the second apostolic age of the Church. We are grateful that we get to see with our own eyes the fulfillment of the prophetic words spoken to us by the forerunners who have gone before us. We agree that we are living in the days of acceleration and that the days of a great harvest are upon us. Release more of Your brilliant presence and let it happen now, even suddenly! We consecrate ourselves unto You for Your purposes and prophetic destiny in the days of the joining of the generations. Send more of Your Spirit now, for Jesus Christ's sake. Amen and amen!*

# ABOUT JAMES W. GOLL

JAMES W. GOLL IS THE FOUNDER OF GOD ENCOUNTERS Ministries—a ministry to the nations. James is a father of four adult children and a growing number of grandchildren. He is the author of over 60 books and study guides, including *The Seer, Dream Language* and *The Lifestyle of a Prophet*. James has his Doctorate from WLI in Practical Ministry and is a Life Language Communications Consultant. James is a recognized voice in the global prayer and prophetic movements, travels the globe in ministry while maintaining his home in Franklin, TN.

# A Coming Revival Greater Than the Charismatic Movement

*Larry Sparks*

The Charismatic Movement of the 1960s and subsequent Jesus People Movement of the '60s and '70s was both glorious and also sobering. It was glorious because of Holy Spirit outpouring, but it was sobering because we witnessed an incomplete picture of what God wanted to do in the earth.

It was so close. We saw renewal and revival, but revival never translated into reformation—a movement where what was taking place in the "church" had a direct, measurable impact on society. Those who came to the Lord were fed a theology that, in many respects, tolerated and celebrated delay. While the church's eyes were looking for a soon-coming Rapture of the church, a generation was being discipled by the influences of darkness in every sphere of influence. Evil laws were passed. Society ran amuck. Education and academia embraced a godless, atheistic philosophy. While the people of God waited to be raptured, the devil saw his opportunity to take nations.

The good news is that God redeems abundantly! Any opportunity for societal transformation that was lost or forfeited in that era can be reclaimed and restored with interest in this present hour. The question is, "What will we do with this glory as we experience it?" Let's explore that, as our stewardship of Holy Spirit outpouring is the very thing that can either extend or break the power of delay.

There is one sure prophetic word concerning the end times that you can stand upon. It's rock solid. In the midst of both dismal prognosticators and enthusiastic futurists, "doom and gloom" skeptics and "everything is getting better" optimists, you can rest on what God Himself said concerning the last days:

> *And in the last days it shall be, God declares, that I will pour out my Spirit on all flesh* (Acts 2:17 ESV).

Since the Day of Pentecost, the Holy Spirit has been released from heaven and has been seeking a compatible resting place on the earth. Yes, all Christians have the Holy Spirit living within them. Theologically we know this. We are regenerated and born again by His effective, supernatural, and sovereign work. At the same time, as Bill Johnson so aptly acknowledges, it's one thing to have the Holy Spirit living within us; it's another dimension to host His presence to such a degree that He rests *upon* us. A groaning creation is not listening for a people who can articulate a solid pneumatology of the Spirit's quickening work in regeneration; they are *looking* for a people whom God visibly rests upon. I believe such a company is coming forth!

## A MOVEMENT THAT MARKED HISTORY WITH HOLY SPIRIT POWER

In the 1960s, a movement took place that radically revolutionized church culture. Church history books record it as the "Charismatic movement" or "Charismatic *Renewal*." Regardless of the language we assign to this epoch season in modern Church history, one thing is for sure—no one was safe from the Holy Spirit in this time of great outpouring. Nearly every denomination and stream of Christianity felt the rumbling of this powerful move of God, which many would trace back to Episcopal priest Dennis Bennett (who recounts his story in the landmark book *9 O'Clock in the Morning*), who got filled with the Holy Spirit, spoke in tongues, and yet continued to operate in his denominational framework. This proceeded to inspire many other Episcopalian believers to contend for Holy Spirit baptism and also legitimized a unique expression of Holy Spirit outpouring where His supernatural work *could function* in a mainline denominational context. You didn't have to become of the Pentecostal tradition to taste of the power of the age to come. From this encounter onward, Lutherans, Baptists, Presbyterians, and Catholics, among many others, experienced a dynamic season of renewal. It was during this period when some of the great ministries and leaders emerged who gave language to the Body of Christ for what God was doing.

God hates division, but He loves uniqueness. During this season of visitation, it didn't matter—pews or chairs, stained glass windows or a living room, organs or a guitar, God was on the move and everything was experiencing fresh life because of His Spirit sweeping through the Church. I believe the Lord is ready to do it again in our day at a level that could make the earth tremble under the weight of God's glory. Are we ready? Are we willing?

## Why Didn't the Glory Sustain and Increase?

I sense such an urgency to prophesy that even though the Charismatic Renewal is to be celebrated and even looked upon as a blueprint for the days in which we are living, that particular season of history did have an element of fault that the Lord is calling us to learn from. This is not a condemnation of what took place; it was glorious and we would do well to contend for such an awakening again today. However, there was a factor that was absent that, I am convinced, limited the reach of what could have happened. We need to learn from our faults. We need to confront the fault of *that* hour so we don't repeat it in ours. And we are awfully close to repeating history if we don't prophetically course correct. We need to be ready, for I prophesy that the Lord is positioning His people for something that will dramatically exceed the impact, influence, and scope of the Charismatic renewal of the 1960s.

> *Repent therefore, and turn back, that your sins may be blotted out, that times of refreshing may come from the presence of the Lord, and that he may send the Christ appointed for you, Jesus, whom heaven must receive until the time for restoring all the things about which God spoke by the mouth of his holy prophets long ago* (Acts 3:19-21 ESV).

### Renewal

In the 1960s, we witnessed the Charismatic Renewal, which was aimed at the Church. The people of God experienced the Holy Spirit in a dynamic new way and thus saw church life infused with His presence and power. In the 1990s, we witnessed renewal with the Toronto Blessing, which became an epicenter of Holy Spirit refreshing for the nations. Believers came from around the world to receive a touch from the Spirit, and in turn we saw many go back to their respective nations or assume their Kingdom assignments and witness millions receive Jesus.

*In this urgent hour in history, I believe the Lord is calling the Church to corporate repentance. Even identificational repentance. Yes, for our sins—but also for the specific sin of rejecting the move of the Holy Spirit and trading it for having a good "Christian" reputation.* The Lord is calling a generation to identificationally undo this trade (made multiple times throughout Church history), repent for being ashamed of the move of the Spirit, and in turn position ourselves for what Malachi prophesied as the Lord coming *suddenly* to His temple (see Mal. 3:1). We need a renewed Church in order to see a revival of souls and a reformation in the land; without the manifest presence of God in our midst, we have little to offer.

## Revival

Repentance *from* the Church will produce refreshing *in* the Church, as witnessed with the Charismatic Renewal, the Toronto Blessing, and other wonderful moves of the Spirit throughout the 1900s. The key is learning how to export our times of refreshing, as the "sound" of a Church experiencing outpouring is meant to summon the masses, as we saw in the book of Acts. The sound of Holy Spirit renewal should never be insulated; a renewed Church should produce revived believers, and revived believers should provoke the unchurched and unsaved to come to Jesus. No, not just "come to church" or come to a meeting, but come to Jesus, and often those who don't know Jesus will be drawn to Him because a revived Christian brought Him into proximity with someone who was asking the question, "Is God really alive?" Renewal should produce a corporate culture in the Church where "word on the street" is that Someone is actually alive and moving in the midst of "those people," the Christians.

*Holy Spirit renewal should always produce revival, where transformed eternal destinies are the fruit.* What's the difference? In the context of my example (the Charismatic Renewal) I see renewal as a time of significant refreshing in the presence of the Lord, as described by the apostle Peter in Acts 3, which gives birth to souls coming into the Kingdom of God.

To recap, in the 1960s you had the Charismatic Renewal, which I am fully convinced gave birth in the spirit to the Jesus Revolution/Jesus People Movement, which was a bona fide revival where countless souls were brought into the Kingdom of God. You had renewal and revival—and many called it quits there. This is what we need to course correct in our day if we are going to see the measure of Kingdom transformation God desires to release into the planet. In the '60s and '70s, people were brought into the Kingdom, but how much of the Kingdom did we see *come out?* I propose to you that "Kingdom come" is measurable. Not by our Christian subculture, but by how those filled with the Spirit of God transform the environments they have been placed in. The *do* of reformation will break the delay that's been causing so much frustration in the ranks of God's people.

## Reformation: the missing key to sustaining revival and seeing societal transformation.

Many could survey the 1960s and '70s and observe a major failure on the Church's part to engage society and culture. In one respect, they would be correct. When the harvest of souls came into the Church during the counter-cultural revolution, as the hippie, free love, and drug culture was being supernaturally invaded by the Holy Spirit, many (mistakenly) assumed this was a sign of a "soon coming" rapture of the Church. Instead of a renewed and revived Church proactively engaging the ills of society (and there were many present and germinating at the time), the people of God retreated into what Dr. Lance Wallnau describes as the "wilderness." Comparatively, this was very much akin to the 40-year wilderness season that the children of Israel found themselves in following their dramatic deliverance from Egypt.

Why did Israel remain in the wilderness when they could have immediately crossed over into the Promised Land? They were intimidated by the enemy tribes who were occupying the land, and they saw this opposition as greater in size and scope than God (the God who just delivered them, supernaturally, from Egyptian bondage through a variety of signs, wonders, and miracles). They saw miracles, but the miracles did not measurably transform their thinking, and we know this because they still saw enemy occupiers as bigger than the God who delivered them. They retreated because their minds were not renewed to think reformationally. Could it be that we are content living in a wilderness with glory, signs, and wonders, when in fact there is so much more that we have been called for? And could it be that our seasons of revival and renewal are short-lived, not because God dispensationally removes His Spirit from the earth but because heaven is seeking a renewed, revived people who steward what they receive in times of outpouring by translating their touch of God into transforming areas of society that have been influenced by the gates of hell.

I prophesy that it's time for the Church to break out of its prolonged wilderness season. Could it be that the reason we have so many conferences, events, glory gatherings, and even our own "Christian culture" is that, maybe, just maybe, we are scared to confront the forces of darkness occupying our nations? We continue to create "other mountains" that separate us from the very clear call of God to give Jesus the nations.

Many are familiar with the concept of the "Seven Mountains of Culture," discussed in part by Loren Cunningham and Bill Bright and then given revelatory expression by Dr. Lance Wallnau. I am absolutely convinced that these seven spheres need to be engaged by renewed and revived people. Arts and Entertainment, Business, Government, Education, Family, Religion, and Politics all make up the "soul of a nation." They are dimensions of created order that are groaning for the influence of the sons and daughters of God who carry the presence of the Spirit. The problem? Instead of raising up a Church to influence these spheres, we continue to create "other mountains" that spiritually insulate us more and more from the very world we are called to impact. Sadly, these are more "spiritual" mountains that place more distance between an already Holy Spirit-filled

Church and a world under the influence of darkness—darkness that must be displaced.

In the 1960s, we witnessed a sobering example of what happens when the Church abdicates the commission to disciple nations. Instead of carrying God's glory and redemptive strategies into law, politics, media, education, and government, the redeemed Ekklesia decided to give itself to having Bible studies, meeting in homes, reading books plotting out end-times scenarios, and watching *Thief in the Night*. Now, while Bible studies, meeting in homes, and attending church services are good and should be encouraged, disengaging from society shouldn't be an option.

*The more the Ekklesia withdraws from society, a demonic and counterfeit version of history will continue to go uncontested and unchallenged. For the Spirit of the Lord is calling a people who would arise, engage, displace the influence of darkness, and proactively write history in agreement with what the Sovereign King has recorded in the Books of Heaven.* God's will *shall* be done in the earth, but the degree that Jesus' Church—His Body, His Bride, His Ekklesia—says "Yes" to the commission to carry and release glory into the ills of society will be the level to which we see the measurable imprint of the Kingdom of God on history. We want to see *His-story* unfold in the earth.

### I Prophesy That It's Time to Come Out of the "Glory Wilderness" and Displace the Darkness Occupying the Promised Land!

In biblical context, the Promised Land was Israel. Our illustrations of any future Promised Lands should never, ever downgrade or displace the significance Israel both had and has to the Lord. For the sake of this illustration, though, I believe the Lord is calling His people out of a wilderness cycle where we've had meetings, services, conferences, and even glory gatherings. We need a "glory gathering" in the high place of media and politics, where leaders marked by the glory of God render decisions or function in creativity because of their connection to the Anointing. We don't need another conference session; we need to learn how to move in and out of the "Counsel of the Lord" when it comes to making decisions for our business. We continue to press in for greater "refreshing" in the Church, but we are not seeing that refreshing translate to the world around us. Why? May our cities, regions, and even nations look different because of the presence of a glorious Church.

The key missing dimension that was absent in the 1960s and '70s was reformation. I am convinced that our gracious God is extending a sovereign opportunity to this generation to see renewal and revival translate into reformation—where society is measurably impacted by the presence of a Spirit-filled, Jesus-exalting, Kingdom-advancing Ekklesia.

During a recent prophetic experience, I was gripped by the following thought: I don't want my daughter, or her children, or her children's children looking back upon this present hour and noticing the absence of the Ekklesia's influence in the pages of history. It's possible for people to miss their day of visitation, as did the vast majority of religious leaders during Jesus' day. They expected one thing, Jesus brought another. Let's be sure that we are building what Jesus wants us to be focusing on in this urgent, strategic, and glorious hour!

## A HAGGAI MOMENT: A CONVERGENCE OF PRIEST, PROPHET, AND GOVERNOR

> *In the second year of Darius the king, in the sixth month, on the first day of the month, the word of the Lord came by the hand of Haggai the prophet to Zerubbabel the son of Shealtiel, governor of Judah, and to Joshua the son of Jehozadak, the high priest* (Haggai 1:1).

For "revival" to translate outside the wilderness of our Charismatic camp and become societal transformation, I see the Lord converging what we see pictured in the book of Haggai—a spiritual alliance of prophet, priest, and government (I think we can expand government to anyone occupying a position of influence in different societal spheres). In our context, here is what I believe the Spirit is saying to the Church right now: In order to build a structure that carries His glory—fashioning a dwelling place for God *in the earth*—there must be intersection in these three realms.

The *prophet,* Haggai, represents the prophetic voice the Lord is raising up in this hour. It's that "messenger anointing" we see pictured in Malachi 3:1, where words of the Lord are released that prepare the way for His "sudden coming" to His temple. It's not one lone-ranger prophet who claims to have a monopoly on hearing from the Lord; this is the opposite of what we will be seeing, so beware and be warned. I see a chorus or collective of prophets functioning in healthy alignment with other expressions of the Church (Ekklesia, fivefold ministry), declaring a word that, although it may have different expressions or attributes, it's calling the people of God into a uniform reality. It's preparatory in nature. It's saying, "If you truly desire a visitation, let alone a habitation of God, in the Church and ultimately in the nations, *this* is how you need to position yourselves." There are things we need to repent of, let go of, and turn away from. Likewise, there are superior realities we need to taste of and turn toward. The prophetic voice of this hour will not be cranky and angry, nor will it be all sunshine and lollypops; this collective of prophets will call the people of God *out of the inferior* for the purpose of calling them into *the superior.*

The *priest* could represent church leaders—those who need to receive and respond to the word of the Lord delivered through the prophetic collective. Why does it seem like we have heard reputable prophetic voices repeating the same words year after year, season after season? The Lord recently showed me that prophets *prophesy.* An obvious revelation, yes, but consider the greater picture. Prophets prophesy. They hear or see, and then give voice to the message they received in the spirit. Why don't we see more prophetic words come to pass? Simple. No one is partnering or participating with them. The "priests"—leaders in the church mountain—need to learn how to respond to prophetic words by partnering with them. God sovereignly gives words to His prophets, but the people of God, particularly church leaders, need to be good stewards of these words, not simply be saying, "I receive that," but by reordering and reorienting life to accommodate the messages from heaven being prophesied.

The *governor* represents seven mountain activism. Just for the record, this is not Christian dominionism, where believers assert themselves as leaders in some kind of societal takeover. I see "dominion" being expressed this way—a company of people filled with the Holy Spirit aim toward ascending the high places of societal influence to assert dominion, not through a natural overthrow but cleansing the spiritual airways and displacing forces of darkness. The one who lives under the Spirit's influence is the one most qualified to have influence. The Lord desires to raise up a company of Spirit-filled leaders who break the cycle of shifting atmospheres.

Right now, Christians have been taught victorious strategies to shift atmospheres that have been under the influence of darkness. We need to study and implement these tools for victorious warfare, yes, but the Lord desires to raise up those who are the ones who set the atmosphere. Yes, the Lord says "set, not shift." Those who ascend the high places will displace darkness, most certainly, but once darkness is dislodged from the high places it's time for those places to be given to the Holy Spirit. This is one way we fulfill the Great Commission. How does Jesus receive nations? We give them to Him. It doesn't always look like us handing countries or continents to Jesus, seeing an entire geography saved. Sometimes, it looks like us stewarding the piece of a nation that we have been given and giving *that* to Jesus.

This actually serves those who are under your influence, be it a company, a nation, or an entire mountain of influence, for I see anointing flowing from the top down. I see the river of God flowing down off those occupying and operating in these "governmental" positions shaping environments of peace, love, joy, gentleness, goodness, and every life-giving attribute that expresses the imminent presence of God's Kingdom. It's about cleansing darkness in the unseen realm so that those in the natural realm directly benefit from environments under Kingdom jurisdiction, for the Kingdom of God is righteousness, peace, and joy in the Holy Spirit (see Rom. 14:17).

*I see righteousness.* What does this look like? First and foremost, it looks like an environment where it's, for lack of a better word, easier for people to discover right standing with God through the work of Jesus. What's all of this seven-mountain, "ascending to the high places" activism really for? One of the key motivations is the creation of environments conducive to people being able to connect with God through Christ Jesus, discovering that the blood of Jesus has made right standing with the Holy God possible. But furthermore, I see the manifestation of righteousness taking place. Righteous decisions. Righteous motives. Righteous—not meaning that the people are perfect, but more that they are operating in harmony with how God Himself would operate in that place.

*I see peace.* What does this look like? The peace of God creates a solid, unshakeable people. In the midst of chaos, individually and societally, in the boardroom and in the headlines, it's possible for people to be anchored in peace. Peace doesn't pretend away problems; it simply rests in the stability of a superior Answer.

*I see joy.* What does this look like? Imagine entire companies, schools, even cities where they are known for *joy*. It is possible. If there could be *"great joy in that city"* in Samaria (Acts 8:8 NKJV), is it possible for us to see this manifestation of joy in our midst today on this same scale—and greater? Yes, because the Holy Spirit who moved in Samaria is the same Spirit moving today. As I reviewed that portion of Scripture, I felt the Lord highlight to me the *why* of joy. Why was there so much joy in that city? The statement in verse 8 has a context:

> *Now those who were scattered went about preaching the word. Philip went down to the city of Samaria and proclaimed to them the Christ. And the crowds with one accord paid attention to what was being said by Philip, when they heard him and saw the signs that he did. For unclean spirits, crying out with a loud voice, came out of many who had them, and many who were paralyzed or lame were healed* (Acts 8:4-7 ESV).

As the enemies of joy were subdued, the city of Samaria was broken open for the Kingdom of God. I see a direct connection between the bold demonstration of signs and wonders and entire cities being opened to receive the Gospel.

This is what it looks like when the Kingdom of God has influence and dominion in spheres of influence—*righteousness, peace, and joy in the Holy Spirit reign!*

For us to see transformation, there must be a threefold convergence of prophet, priest, and governor; otherwise, we will continue to believe and perpetuate the lie that the ultimate expression of God's movement is renewal in the church and revival among the lost. There is a third dimension that determines the destinies of nations. How will the move of God be translated into government, education, arts and entertainment, business, politics, and every other sphere of influence? This is our assignment—when we translate God's movement outside of the church walls and into society, we will see delay broken and Kingdom purposes established!

## Encountering the Terror and Awe of Jehovah Sabaoth

I was reluctant to even include this as part of the prophetic word, but I just heard the word *motivation*. What motivates us to carry the move of the Spirit outside of the church, let alone host His presence in our gatherings? The fear of the Lord.

There seems to be a connection between building the house of God and the identity of the Lord as Jehovah Sabaoth, *the Lord of Hosts*. I cannot provide full articulation to this right now. All I know is that in the days ahead, the Lord is going to unveil Himself to us as the "Lord of Angel Armies" in a new, powerful way. There is a direct link between this identity of God and a people who tremble under holy awe and fear. It's a weightiness of divine presence that we have yet to taste of in our 21st century church culture. We've had glimpses, for sure. Throughout revival history, we see account after account of God "coming" with heaviness during periods of awakening. I sense the Lord bringing a normality to this manifestation of divine presence where everything shifts and we become immediately aware that we are in the presence of the One who commands the host of heaven. He commands them and, likewise, He comes with them.

"For My people to go up, they need to grow up." The Lord spoke this to me recently concerning the unseen realm and how Christians should become better acquainted with the activity of the spirit world. We live so disconnected from the concept of an invisible realm, and yet, every day, we experience the results, both in our lives and in our world, of society being influenced by the invisible realm. This is actually the realm everything in the physical was birthed out of. Before creation, there wasn't nothing; there was an invisible realm. First, there was God; second, there was the realm where God dwelt and operated. In this realm are angels. There are heavenly hosts. There are demons and forces aimed at displacing or disrupting Kingdom advancement. There is much activity in the unseen realm. Many Christians, even Spirit-filled believers, run from it out of fear that we will become distracted by it and start worshiping angels or talking with the dead. To retreat in fear is actually falling right into the enemy's agenda, as he would love nothing more than to own the airways. To the degree that we live disconnected from the invisible realm, we will continue to give the enemy influence over the airways. It's time to arise, recognizing the Jehovah Sabaoth leads the charge! It's time for us to discover how to partner with God's invisible activity while keeping our eyes fixed on Jesus.

Furthermore, Jehovah Sabaoth is a name that invokes the weight and majesty of God. We've taught the redemptive names of God in a unique context; we often present God's names as expressions of what He *does* for us. He's our healer, our provider, our shepherd, the One who sees us, so on and so forth. When we encounter the Lord of Hosts, it's not for our bene-fit. He's not coming to give us something; He's coming with His hosts and His armies, seeking partners in the earth realm. He's coming to accom-plish His purposes, as He revealed to Joshua in Joshua 5:14.

I believe we need to welcome the Lord of Hosts, the God of Angel Armies, in our midst. We need to recognize His movement and respond in holy awe. And if we are truly desiring heaven to come to earth, we need to be willing to expand our thinking on what this invasion from another realm looks like—and who accompanies it. Angels. The cloud of wit-nesses. Spiritual activity in the heavenly realms. I recognize some people talk about such things freely and irreverently. It almost sounds like some Charismatic free-for-all. How can you recognize the pure and genuine? Those who encounter the realms of heaven, and the corresponding activ-ity in these dimensions, carry a trembling of the Lord on their lips. Every being in heaven, measured next to the One upon the Throne, is infinitely inferior in glory, wonder, and majesty. We are not worshiping angels, we are not seeking to communicate with saints in heaven, we are not allow-ing our eyes to be distracted from being fixed upon Jesus. We are simply learning how to operate in these supernatural realms so that the invisible realm of the Kingdom influences the visible.

## A People Who Move In and Out of Mount Zion—Breaking Delay in Divine Encounter!

Many people pray for God to "come down." I understand the language and grasp the purpose of such a prayer—for us to experience the manifest presence of the Spirit in our immediate context. Unfortunately, this well-meaning language can perpetuate delay in our lives when it comes to encountering the presence of the Lord. We feel the frustration of "delay" in our personal relationship with God because we are perpetually waiting for Him to "come down" and "visit" us when, in fact, this already happened with Jesus. Furthermore, the work of Jesus broke the wait. The cross of Christ, the sprinkled blood on the mercy seat of heaven, and subsequent outpouring of the Spirit broke every single delay to the people of God engaging His presence.

Let me give you an example. While driving to Bethel Church in Redding, I was driving up a mountain, as the main campus sits on a stunning hilltop. As I went up the mountain, I prayed, "God, would You come and meet us here today," in preparation for the church service. I felt the immediate interruption of the Lord calling me to reconsider my language. I sensed Him telling me to stop waiting for Him to come down and instead, on the basis of His blood, "Ascend."

> *You have come to Mount Zion, to the city of the living God, the heavenly Jerusalem, and to countless thousands of angels in a joyful gathering* (Hebrews 12:22 NLT).

In the same way I was ascending the hill in Redding, California to get to the church, I have access to ascend the "hill" of Mount Zion in the spirit realm and engage the manifest presence of God anytime—not just when I perceive He has "come down." This place of encounter with God is the inheritance of every single born-again believer, as the blood of Jesus has given you spirit-to-Spirit access into the Most Holy Place. The writer of Hebrews refers to it as Mount Zion, contrasting it previously with Mount Sinai, a place that was limited and exclusive. Under the Old Testament, only Moses could ascend; because of the New Covenant in Jesus' blood, you have the right to ascend a hill called Zion, encounter the One whose eyes burn like fire, and instantly translate your encounter with the King of Glory into whatever sphere you have been called to influence.

This statement, I believe, is meant to conclude this prophetic word. God is seeking a company of people who learn how to move seamlessly in and out of Zion, the realm of divine presence and encounter. One moment, they are in Zion, the next, leading in the boardroom. One moment, they are in His glory, the next, they are drafting bills, laws, and ordinances. One moment, they are enraptured in the secret place with Father God, the next, they are writing a screenplay. One moment, they are in the Counsel of the Lord, hearing the thunder of His Throne room; the next, they are speaking before the Board of Education about future curriculum.

How do you *ascend?* By faith. More often than not, you won't feel worthy or qualified to enter God's presence. Here is what you need to remember: you cannot enter God's presence on any merit of your own. Not your thoughts, your feelings, your good works, your church attendance, how "good" you did today, or how "bad" you slipped. You ascend and enter into God's presence on the basis of the blood of Jesus. *"On the basis of My blood."* I hear the Lord thundering that declaration over you, as the very place you were born to function in, Mount Zion, is the very place the enemy works the hardest to keep you out of.

> *Let us then with confidence draw near to the throne of grace,*
> *that we may receive mercy and find grace to help in time of*
> *need* (Hebrews 4:16 ESV).

Your confidence is not in yourself; your ability to draw near is strictly in the merit of Jesus' blood. The powerful reality is that by faith, you initiate the process. God did His part through the work of Jesus and the Day of Pentecost. God sovereignly drew near first; now, it's your turn. Respond in faith to the work of Jesus and the outpouring of the Spirit. Note the words of the author of Hebrews. There is nothing to suggest that we wait around for God to "come down." Consider the invitation starts with, *"Let us then with confidence draw near."* James (Jacob) puts it this way: *"Draw near to God, and he will draw near to you"* (James 4:8 ESV).

These encounters all begin with an earth-to-heaven initiative. The enemy will try to do everything possible to distract us from boldly entering into His presence, particularly using the lies of guilt and shame. Both are rightly identified as "lies" because neither guilt nor shame determine our eligibility to enter into the presence of God; only the blood of Jesus does. And the very things we need to combat guilt and shame are found in the presence, at the *throne of grace*. We need to receive mercy, which reminds us of our right standing with God through the work of Jesus, and we also access grace to help or empower us to have victory over our areas of weakness and need. Both of these essentials (grace and mercy) are found in one place—the throne of grace, a realm of proximity to God that we are summoned to approach with boldness and confidence!

God wants to bring reformation to nations—that's ultimately the heartbeat behind this prophetic word. Yet in order for us to carry something into nations that displaces darkness and influences culture, we first need to be a people who live *under the influence*. To do this, I am convinced Christians need to be a company of people who seamlessly move in and out of Zion. They move in as lovers of God who become saturated in His glory, and they move out as activists who release measurable Kingdom advancement in their respective spheres of influence.

What was so special about October 6, the day I received this prophetic word about "No more delay"? Simple. I wasn't looking for this word. As mentioned earlier, I was convinced there were other people out there communicating this message more effectively than me. Then I realized there was something holy and urgent on it. My friend, prophet Lana Vawser, texted me the evening of October 6, 2018, simply informing me to look up Revelation 10:6. These are the words that gripped my heart, confirming that this word of "No more delay" was something heaven was thundering:

> *He swore an oath in the name of the one who lives forever and ever, who created the heavens and everything in them, the earth and everything in it, and the sea and everything in it. He said, "**There will be no more delay**"* (Revelation 10:6 NLT).

Heaven is presently thundering "No more delay!"

It's time to seize the moment we have been entrusted with and ensure that when the history books concerning this period in history are written, future generations would see the definable imprint of the Ekklesia!

# ABOUT LARRY SPARKS

LARRY SPARKS IS PUBLISHER FOR DESTINY IMAGE (DESTINYIMAGE .com), a Spirit-filled publishing house pioneered by Don Nori, Sr. in 1983 with a mandate to publish the prophets. Larry is fueled by a vision to help the church community create space for the Holy Spirit to move in freedom, power, and revival fire, providing every believer with an opportunity to have a life-changing encounter in the presence of God. In addition to publishing, Larry is a regular contributor to *Charisma* magazine; he conducts seminars on revival; hosts regional Renewing South Florida gatherings; and has been featured on Sid Roth's *It's Supernatural!*, TBN, CBN, the ElijahList, and Cornerstone TV. He is also on the leadership team of International Young Prophets. Larry earned a Master of Divinity from Regent University and enjoys life in Texas with his beautiful wife and beloved daughter.

You can connect with him at:

Facebook.com/larryvsparks

lawrencesparks.com